Contents

I. INTRODUCTION: The Unconscious and its Language

Waking Up to the Unconscious

One morning a woman got into her car as usual and drove several miles to her office. Along the way her imagination began to produce a great adventure. She saw herself in olden times, a simple woman living in the midst of wars and crusades. She became a heroine, saved her people by strength and sacrifice, encountered a strong and noble prince who loved her.

With her conscious mind thus totally occupied, she drove along several streets, stopped at traffic lights, signaled properly at each turn, and arrived safely at her office parking lot. Coming to her senses, she realized that she couldn't remember any of the drive to the office. She recalled not a single intersection or turn. Her startled mind asked: "How could I drive this far without being aware of it? Where was my mind? Who was driving while I was dreaming?" But things like that had happened before, so she dropped the subject and went on into the office.

At her desk she began to plan her day's work, but she was interrupted by a colleague who came storming into her office, threw down a memorandum she had circulated, and went into a rage over some minor point he disagreed with. She was astonished. His anger was so disproportionate to the size of the issue! What had come over him?

He, in turn, hearing his own raised voice, realized he was making a mountain out of a molehill. Embarrassed, he mumbled an apology and backed out. In his own office he asked himself: "What came over me? Where did that come from? I don't usually get rattled over little things. I just wasn't *myself!*" He sensed that there was a boiling anger within him that had nothing to do with his friend's memorandum but had suddenly come to the surface over this petty matter. Where the anger came from, he didn't know.

If these two people had time to think about it, they might realize that they had already felt the presence of the unconscious in their lives that morning. In dozens of ways in the ebb and flow of ordinary daily life, we experience the unconscious as it acts in us and through us.

Sometimes it works alongside the conscious mind and takes over the controls of the automobile while the conscious mind is focused on something else. We have all had the experience of driving a few blocks on "automatic pilot" as the woman in our example did. The conscious mind is somewhere else, briefly, and the unconscious mind simply takes over whatever we are doing. It stops us at the red lights, starts us at the green lights, and keeps us within the law until the conscious mind comes back to the here-and-now. This isn't the safest way to drive, but the unconscious does provide us with an excellent, and crucial, built-in back-up system that we all take for granted.

Sometimes the unconscious generates a fantasy so full of vivid, symbolic images that it captures the conscious mind totally and holds our attention for a long time. The fantasy of adventure, danger, heroic sacrifice, and love that enthralled the woman on her way to work is a primary example of the way the unconscious invades our conscious minds and attempts to express itself—through the *imagination*, using the symbolic language of feeling-charged images.

Another way we experience the unconscious is through a sudden surge of emotion, the inexplicable joy or the irrational anger that suddenly invades the conscious mind and takes it over. The floods of feeling make no sense to the conscious mind, because the conscious mind did not produce them. The man in our example could not explain to himself the intensity of his reaction. He asked, "Where did that come from?" He felt that his anger came from somewhere *outside* him. He felt that he was "not himself" for a few moments. But in fact this surge of ungovernable emotion did come from a part of him, a place deep within that he couldn't see with his conscious mind. It is because of this invisibility that this place within is called the "unconscious."

The idea of the unconscious derives from a simple observation in daily human life: There is material contained in our minds that we are not aware of most of the time. We sometimes become aware of a memory, a pleasant association, an ideal, a belief that wells up unexpectedly from an unknown place. We sense that we have carried these elements somewhere inside us for a long time—but where? In an unknown part of the total psyche that lies outside the boundaries of the conscious mind.

The unconscious is a marvelous universe of unseen energies, forces, forms of intelligence—even distinct *personalities*—that live within us. It is a much larger realm than most of us realize, one that has a complete life of its own running parallel to the ordinary life we live day to day. The unconscious is the secret source of much of our thought, feeling, and behavior. It influences us in ways that are all the more powerful because unsuspected.

Most of us have an intuitive feeling about what is meant when we hear the term the *unconscious*. We correlate this idea with myriads of experiences, small and large, that are interwoven with the fabric of our daily lives. We all have had the experience of doing something unconsciously when our minds were "someplace else," then being surprised at what we had done. We remember getting worked up during a conversation and blurting out some strong opinion we didn't know consciously that we held.

Sometimes we are startled: "Where did that come from? I didn't know I felt so strongly about that." As we become more sensitive to the surges of energy from the unconscious we learn instead to ask, "What *part of me* believes that? Why does this subject set off such an intense reaction in that unseen part of myself?"

We can learn to look at the issue more closely. What "comes over me" is a sudden invasion of energy from the unconscious. If I think I wasn't being "myself," it is because I don't realize that "myself" also includes my unconscious. These hidden parts of ourselves have strong feelings and want to express them. Yet, unless we learn to do *inner work*, these parts of ourselves are hidden from our conscious view.

Sometimes these hidden personalities are embarrassing or violent, and we are humiliated when they show themselves. At other times we wake up to strengths and fine qualities within ourselves that we never knew were there. We draw on hidden resources and do things we normally could not have done, say something more clear and intelligent than we've ever been able to say before, express wisdom we did not know we had, show a generosity or understanding of which we never knew we were capable. In each case there is a startled reaction: "I am a different person than I thought I was. I have qualities—both positive and negative—that

I didn't know were part of my definition." These qualities lived in the unconscious, where they were "out of sight, out of mind."

We are all much more than the "I" of whom we are aware. Our conscious minds can focus on only a limited sector of our total being at any given time. Despite our efforts at self-knowledge, only a small portion of the huge energy system of the unconscious can be incorporated into the conscious mind or function at the conscious level. Therefore we have to learn how to go to the unconscious and become receptive to its messages: It is the only way to find the unknown parts of ourselves.

APPROACHING THE UNCONSCIOUS—VOLUNTARILY OR INVOLUNTARILY

The unconscious manifests itself through a language of symbols. It is not only in our involuntary or compulsive behavior that we can see the unconscious. It has two natural pathways for bridging the gap and speaking to the conscious mind: One is by *dreams*; the other is through the *imagination*. Both of these are highly refined channels of communication that the psyche has developed so that the unconscious and conscious levels may speak to one another and work together.

The unconscious has developed a special language to use in dreams and imagination: It is the language of symbolism. As we will see, inner work is primarily the art of learning this symbolic language of the unconscious. Therefore we will devote most of our time to working with dreams, imagination, and the uses of symbolism.

Many communicative efforts by the unconscious are lost on us. The unconscious bubbles to the surface in dreams, but few people have the information necessary to take their dreams seriously and understand their language. The activity of the unconscious is also evident in the running of the imagination: the bursts of fantasy that float like bubbles across the landscape of the conscious mind, barely noticed by us; the veritable floods of fantasy that seize many people regularly and run like rivers along the edges of their minds. We think we are "thinking" or we think we are "planning," but more often we are in a daydream, lost for a few minutes in that stream of fantasy before we pull ourselves back to the physical situation, the work at hand, the persons with whom we are speaking.

To get a true sense of who we are, become more complete and integrated human beings, we must go to the unconscious and set up communication with it. Much of ourselves and many determinants of our character are contained in the unconscious. It is only by approaching it that we have a chance to become conscious, complete, whole human beings. Jung has shown that by approaching the unconscious and learning its symbolic language, we live richer and fuller lives. We begin to live in partnership with the unconscious rather than at its mercy or in constant warfare with it.

Most people, however, do not approach the unconscious voluntarily. They only become aware of the unconscious when they get into trouble with it. We modern people are so out of touch with the inner world that we encounter it mostly through psychological distress. For example, a woman who thinks she has everything under control may find herself horribly depressed, able neither to shake it off nor to understand what is happening to her. Or a man may find that he has terrible conflicts between the life he lives outwardly and the unconscious ideals he holds deep inside himself where he never looks. He feels torn or anxiety-ridden, but can't say why.

When we experience inexplicable conflicts that we can't resolve; when we become aware of urges in ourselves that seem irrational, primitive, or destructive; when a neurosis afflicts us because our conscious attitudes are at odds with our instinctual selves—then we begin to realize that the unconscious is playing a role in our lives and we need to face it.

Historically, it was through this kind of pathology that Jung and Freud rediscovered the existence of the unconscious—through the psychological suffering of patients in whom the relationship between the conscious and unconscious levels had broken down.

JUNG'S MODEL OF THE UNCONSCIOUS

Jung discovered that the unconscious is not merely an appendage of the conscious mind, a place where forgotten memories or unpleasant feelings are repressed. He posited a model of the untonscious so momentous that the Western world has still not fully caught up with its implications. He showed that the unconscious is the creative source of all that evolves into the conscious mind and into the total personality of each individual. It is out of the raw material of the unconscious that our conscious minds develop, mature, and expand to include all the qualities that we carry potentially within us. It is from this treasure trove that we are enriched with strengths and qualities we never knew we possessed.

Jung showed us that the conscious and the unconscious minds both have critical roles to play in the equilibrium of the total self. When they are out of correct balance with one another, neurosis or other disturbances result.

THE EVOLUTION OF CONSCIOUSNESS

Jung's studies and work led him to conclude that the unconscious is the real source of all our human consciousness. It is the source of our human capacity for orderly thought, reasoning, human awareness, and feeling. The unconscious is the Original Mind of humankind, the primal matrix out of which our species has evolved a conscious mind and then developed it over the millennia to the extent and the refinement that it has today. Every capacity, every feature of our functioning consciousness, was first contained in the unconscious and then found its way from there up to the conscious level.

Jung developed a magnificent vision of this human capacity for consciousness, of its role and meaning. He saw a creative force at work in nature—a cosmos laboring through timeless aeons to give birth to this rare quality that we call consciousness. Through the human race, the huge unconscious psyche of Nature has slowly made a part of itself conscious. Jung believed that God and all of creation labored through time to bring conscious awareness into the universe, and that it is the role of human beings to carry that evolution forward.

Human consciousness develops out of the primal matter of the unconscious. Its growth is nourished by a continuing stream of contents from the unconscious that rises gradually to the level of consciousness, seeking to form a more complete, conscious person. The incorporation of unconscious materials must continue until, finally, the conscious mind reflects the wholeness of the total self.

Jung believed that every mortal has an individual role to play in this evolution. For just as our collective human capacity for consciousness evolved out of the unconscious psyche, so it does in each individual. Each of us must, in an individual lifetime, recapitulate the evolution of the human race, and each of us must be an individual container in which the evolution of consciousness is carried forward.

Each of us is a microcosm in which the universal process actualizes itself. Therefore we are all caught up in the movement of the contents of the unconscious toward the level of the conscious mind. Each of us is involved in the countermovement of the ego-mind back toward the unconscious, reconnecting with its root in the parent matrix that gave it its birth.

Within the unconscious of each person is the primal pattern, the "blueprint," if you will, according to which the conscious mind and the total functional personality are formed—from birth through all the slow years of psychological growth toward genuine inner maturity. This pattern, this invisible latticework of energy, contains all the traits, all the strengths, the faults, the basic structure and parts that will make up a total psychological being.

In most of us, only a small portion of this storehouse of raw energy has been assimilated into the conscious personality. Only a small part of the original blueprint has been actualized at the conscious level.

The inner, unconscious model of the individual is like the plan for a cathedral: At first, as the plan is translated into physical reality, only the general contours can be seen. After a time, a small part of the actual structure is finished enough to give an intimation of what the final work of art will be. As years pass the edifice rises, stone by stone, until finally the last blocks are in place and the finishing touches are complete. Only then is the magnificent vision of the architect revealed.

In the same way, the true depth and grandeur of an individual human being is never totally manifested until the main elements of the personality are moved from the level of potential in the unconscious and actualized at the level of conscious functioning.

Each of us is building a life, building an edifice. Within each person the plan and the basic structure are established in a deep place in the unconscious. But we need to consult the unconscious and cooperate with it in order to realize the full potential that is built into us. And we have to face the challenges and painful changes that the process of inner growth always brings.

THE EGO IN THE MIDST OF THE UNCONSCIOUS

The unconscious is an enormous field of energy, much larger than the conscious mind. Jung compared the ego—the conscious mind—to a cork bobbing in the enormous ocean of the unconscious. He also compared the conscious mind to the tip of an iceberg that rises above the surface of the water. Ninety-five percent of an iceberg is hidden beneath the dark, icy waters. The unconscious, like most of the iceberg, is out of sight. But it is enormously powerful—and as dangerous as a submerged iceberg if not respected. More people have sunk after collisions with the unconscious than *Titanics* after collisions with icebergs.

Ego, in Latin, simply means "I." Freud and Jung referred to the conscious mind as the *ego* because this is the part of the psyche that calls itself "I," that is "self-conscious"—aware of itself as a being, as a field of energy that is independent and distinct from others. When we say "I" we are referring to only that small sector of ourselves of which we are aware. We assume that "I" contains only *this* personality, *these* traits, *these* values and viewpoints that are up on the surface within the ego's range of vision, accessible to consciousness. This is my limited, highly inaccurate version of who "I" am.

The ego-mind is not aware that the total "I" is much larger, more extensive than the ego, that the part of the psyche that is hidden in the unconscious is much greater than the conscious mind and much more powerful.

Our egos tend to think of the unconscious as being outside ourselves, even though its contents are actually deep inside us. This is why we hear people say things like "I just wasn't myself when I did that." When we find ourselves doing something unexpected, something that doesn't fit in with our conscious conception of ourselves, we speak of it as though someone else were acting rather than ourselves. The conscious mind is startled, because it pretends that the unconscious isn't there. Since the total psyche is much larger and more complex than the ego-mind can grasp, these unexpected things always feel as though they come from outside us rather than from within us.

In dreams and myths the conscious mind is often symbolized by an island. Like an island people in an island world, the ego sets up a little world of its own—a system of order and a set of assumptions about reality. Our egos are not aware that outside the limits of their little islands, outside the narrow perimeters of their vision, there is a whole universe of realities and truths contained in the vast sea of the unconscious that our egos can't perceive.

Deep in this unseen ocean of energy huge forces are at work. Mythical kingdoms, symbolized by the legends of Atlantis, exist there in the depths and carry on lives parallel to the daily life of our conscious minds. Centers of alternative consciousness, alternative values, attitudes, and ideas exist there like other islands in the great sea. They wait to be discovered and acknowledged by the searching conscious mind.

The purpose of learning to work with the unconscious is not just to resolve our conflicts or deal with our neuroses. We find there a deep source of renewal, growth, strength, and wisdom. We connect with the source of our evolving character; we cooperate with the process whereby we bring the total self together; we learn to tap that rich lode of energy and intelligence that waits within.

THE UNCONSCIOUS AND THE INNER LIFE

The *inner life* that Jung described is the secret life we all lead, by day and night, in constant companionship with our unseen, unconscious, inner selves. When human life is in balance, the conscious mind and the unconscious live in relationship. There is a constant flow of energy and information between the two levels as they meet in the dimension of dream, vision, ritual, and imagination.

The disaster that has overtaken the modern world is the complete splitting off of the conscious mind from its roots in the unconscious. All the forms of interaction with the unconscious that nourished our ancestors—dream, vision, ritual, and religious experience—are largely lost to us, dismissed by the modern mind as primitive or superstitious. Thus, in our pride and hubris, our faith in our unassailable reason, we cut ourselves off from our origins in the unconscious and from the deepest parts of ourselves.

In modern Western society we have reached a point at which we try to get by without acknowledging the inner life at all. We act as though there were no unconscious, no realm of the soul, as though we could live full lives by fixating ourselves completely on the external, material world. We try to deal with all the issues of life by external means—making more money, getting more power, starting a love affair, or "accomplishing something" in the material world. But we discover to our surprise that the inner world is a reality that we ultimately have to face.

Jung observed that most of the neurosis, the feeling of fragmentation, the vacuum of meaning, in modern lives, results from this isolation of the ego-mind from the unconscious. As conscious beings we all go about with a vague sense that we have lost a part of ourselves, that something that once belonged to us is missing.

Our isolation from the unconscious is synonymous with our isolation from our souls, from the life of the spirit. It results in the loss of our religious life, for it is in the unconscious that we find our individual conception of God and experience our deities. The religious function—this inborn demand for meaning and inner experience—is cut off with the rest of the inner life. And it can only *force* its way back into our lives through neurosis, inner conflicts, and psychological symptoms that demand our attention.

Several years ago I was invited to speak at a Roman Catholic seminary. At the last minute some mischievous urge took hold of me and I entitled my lecture "Your Neurosis as a Low-grade Religious Experience." The lecture apparently shook the congregation profoundly. I had a greater deluge of questions, impassioned conversations, and raised voices than I had ever had. The subject touched a raw nerve, you see. People were startled to hear that if we don't go to the spirit, the spirit comes to us as neurosis. This is the immediate, practical connection between psychology and religion in our time.

Every person must live the inner life in one form or another. Consciously or unconsciously, voluntarily or involuntarily, the inner world will claim us and exact its dues. If we go to that realm consciously, it is by our *inner work*: our prayers, meditations, dream work, ceremonies, and Active Imagination. If we try to ignore the inner world, as most of us do, the unconscious will find its way into our lives through pathology: our psychosomatic symptoms, compulsions, depressions, and neuroses.

THE PROCESS OF INDIVIDUATION

Individuation is the term Jung used to refer to the lifelong process of becoming the complete human beings we were born to be. Individuation is our waking up to our total selves, allowing our conscious personalities to develop until they include all the basic elements that are inherent in each of us at the preconscious level. This is the "actualizing of the blueprint" of which we spoke earlier.

Why should this be called "individuation"? Because this process of actualizing oneself and becoming more complete also reveals one's special, individual structure. It shows how the universal human traits and possibilities are combined in each individual in a way that is unlike anyone else.

Jung emphasized the uniqueness of each person's psychological structure. Thus, the name he gave this process was not an accident; it reflected his conviction that the more one faces the unconscious and makes a synthesis between its contents and what is in the conscious mind, the more one derives a sense of one's unique individuality.

At the same time, individuation does not mean becoming isolated from the human race. Once we feel more secure as individuals, more complete within ourselves, it is natural also to seek the myriad ways in which we resemble our fellow human beings—the values, interests, and essentially human qualities that bind us together in the human tribe. If we look closely, we see that our individuality consists in the special way that we combine the universal psychological patterns and energy systems that all human beings have in common. Jung called these patterns the *archetypes*.

Since the archetypes are universal, they are all present in the unconscious of each person. But they combine in infinite variations to create individual human psyches. We may compare all this to the physical human body. In some ways our bodies are like those of all other human beings. We all have arms, legs, hearts, livers, and skin in one form or another. They are universal characteristics of the human species. Yet, if I compare my fingerprints or strands of my hair with those of other people, I find that no two human bodies are exactly alike.

In the same way the universal psychological energies and capacities in the human race are combined differently in each of us. Each person has a distinct psychological structure. It is only by living that inherent structure that one discovers what it means to be an individual.

If we work at individuation, we begin to see the difference between the ideas and values that come out of our own selves and the social opinions that we absorb from the world around us. We can cease to be mere appendages of a society or a clique of people: We learn that we have our own values, our own ways of life, that proceed naturally out of our inborn natures.

A great sense of security develops from this process of individuation. One begins to understand that it isn't necessary to struggle to be like someone else, for by being one's own self one stands on the surest ground. We realize that to know ourselves completely and to develop all the strengths that are built into us is a lifetime task. We don't need to make an imitation of someone else's life. There is no further need for pretensions, for what is already ours is riches enough, and far more than we ever expected.

Inner Work: Seeking the Unconscious

The purpose of this book is to provide a practical, step-by-step approach to doing your own inner work. Specifically, you will find a four-step method for both dream work and Active Imagination. As part of our exploration we will also touch on the uses of ceremony and fantasy as avenues into the unconscious.

I refer to these techniques as "inner work" because they are direct, powerful ways of approaching the inner world of the unconscious. Inner work is the effort by which we gain awareness of the deeper layers of consciousness within us and move toward integration of the total self.

A practical approach is needed, regardless of how sophisticated we may be on the theoretical level. Though all of us have been exposed to a number of psychological theories, few have a sense of how to get started in actually working with dreams and with the unconscious. Usually our energy stays where it started, on the level of theory, and does not translate into a concrete, immediate encounter with the inner self.

In the world of psyche, it is your *work*, rather than your theoretical ideas, that builds consciousness. If we go to our own dreams and sincerely work with the symbols that we find there, we generally learn most of what we need to know about ourselves and the meaning of our lives, regardless of how much we know of the psychological theories involved.

The point of inner work is to build consciousness. By learning to do your own inner work, you gain insight into the conflicts and challenges that your life presents. You are able to search the hidden depths of your own unconscious to find the strengths and resources that wait to be discovered there.

Actually, any form of meditation that opens our minds to the messages of the unconscious can be called "inner work." Humankind has developed an infinite variety of approaches to the inner world, each adapted to a stage of history, a culture, a religion, or a view of our relationship to the spirit. A few examples are yogic meditation, *zazen* in Zen Buddhism, Christian contemplative prayer, the meditations on the life of Christ practiced by Thomas à Kempis and Ignatius of Loyola, Sufi meditation, and ethical meditation in Confucian philosophy.

Jung observed that the the aboriginal people of Australia spend *two-thirds* of their waking lives in some form of inner work. They do religious ceremony, discuss and interpret their dreams, make spirit quests, "go walkabout." All this consistent effort is devoted to the inner life, to the realm of dreams, totems, and spirits—that is, to making contact with the unconscious. We modern people can scarcely get a few hours free in an entire week to devote to the inner world. This is why, for all our technology, we may know less of our souls and less of God than seemingly primitive people do.

But there is another basic difference between us and aboriginal peoples: They have held on to their ancient forms of worship and of approaching the inner world. When they choose to go to the spirit, there is a prescribed way to do the spirit quest, a prescribed way to understand the dreams and visions, a prescribed ceremony for meeting the gods in the magic circle or at the altar. For us, most of the old ways are gone. Those of us who want to learn once again how to walk in the Land of Dreaming, to communicate with the great spirits, have to learn afresh how to go to our dreams, how to rekindle ancient fires from the energy of the unconscious, how to reawaken tribal memories long forgotten. We have to go to a modern-day shaman like Carl Jung to find a way to the soul that makes sense to our modern mind.

The forms of inner work that we will explore are based on the teachings and insights of Jung. Dream work is derived, of course, from Jungian dream analysis. It involves learning to read the symbolic language of dreams. Active Imagination is a special way of using the power of the imagination to develop a working relationship between the conscious mind and the unconscious. It is an age-old process that Jung reformulated into a technique that modern people could use.

Active Imagination is not like some current "visualization" techniques in which one imagines something with a goal in mind. There is no script; Active Imagination has a completely different relationship with the unconscious, one based on recognition of its reality and power. In Active Imagination, you go to your unconscious to find out what is there and to learn what it has to offer to the conscious mind. The unconscious is not something to be manipulated to suit the purposes of the conscious mind, but an equal partner to engage in dialogue that leads to a fuller maturity.

Many people are aware that the unconscious communicates to our conscious minds through dreams. Many have learned theories about how to interpret dreams. But most of us become paralyzed when we try to work with our own specific dreams. Here is a familiar scenario: I awaken with a vivid dream. I decide to try to "do it on my own." I dutifully write the dream in my notebook. I sit down to "interpret." Suddenly my mind goes blank. I ask myself: "What am I supposed to do? Where do I start?" I stare at the page. The dream seems either completely obvious or utterly meaningless.

Sometimes we make a stab at finding some associations for the dream images. But we lose patience. We sense that we have missed the point. We decide to come back another day and try again, but by then other things have claimed us.

In the early years of my work I found that this was a universal problem among patients and friends. Somehow, no matter how much we read about the theories of dream symbolism, we all get stuck when it comes to the practical, immediate job of working on our own dreams. People were coming to the consulting room with notebooks filled with dreams. When I asked what they had learned from the dreams, they would say: "I don't understand it. When I am here during my analytical hour, we get such revelations from my dreams. But when I sit down by myself to work on them, I don't see anything. I don't know where to start."

Getting started on one's own dreams is not a problem only for laypeople; it is equally a problem for most psychologists. When I work with patients' dreams, I may shine, but when it is my own dream, my mind short-circuits. This is normal, for each dream communicates information that isn't known consciously by the dreamer. It therefore takes some real effort, some stretching of our capacities, to get a hold on what the dream is saying. If the interpretation comes too easily, it is not likely to be as accurate or as deep.

In response to this practical need, I began to develop the four-step approach to dreams that you will find in this book. My goal is to provide a way for people to interpret dreams on their own. Most people need to learn how to go to their own dreams, their own unconscious, for their authority. But, in order to do this, we need a practical approach that gets us started: a series of physical and mental steps that enable us to approach the dream, break it down into symbols, and discover the meanings that these symbols have for us.

Since the time, years ago, when I and my patients developed the four-step method, I have observed that most people who use it conscientiously can get at the real substance of their dreams and arrive at a fairly accurate interpretation. They find the essence or main energy of their dreams, and that is what is important.

An overinvolvement with theories is a main obstacle to dream work:

Naturally, a doctor must be familiar with the so-called "methods." But he must guard against falling into any specific, routine approach. In general one must guard against theoretical assumptions. . . . To my mind, in dealing with individuals, only individual understanding will do. We need a different language for every patient. In one analysis I can be heard talking the Adlerian dialect, in another the Freudian. (Jung, *MDR*, p. 131)*

From Jung I took courage to tell my patients not to put their faith in abstract concepts. Put your faith in your own unconscious, your own dreams. If you would learn from your dreams, then work with them. Live with the symbols in your dreams as though they were your physical companions in daily life. You will discover, if you do, that they really are your companions in the inner world.

ANALYSIS AND HOMEWORK

This book is not intended to substitute for the help and guidance of your analyst if you are doing formal analysis. But it is in-

---

Memories, Dreams and Reflections will be designated throughout with this abbreviation. Other works of Jung will be referred to by the abbreviation *CW*, for *Collected Works*, preceded by volume number and followed by paragraph number. To eliminate footnotes as much as possible, all quotations will be followed in the text by the author's name and short title only. The complete references for all materials quoted will be found in the Bibliography.

tended to help you with your homework. You should discuss the approaches that you find here and follow your analyst's advice in using these techniques.

People get the best out of analysis when they do their homework day by day and bring their dreams, fantasy material, and Active Imagination to the therapist after they have worked on it and partially "digested" it. The analytical hour can then be spent on refining or amplifying the work that has already been done. This allows the analyst to make the best use of the patient's time and helps the patient to develop at a faster pace.

WORKING WITHOUT AN ANALYST

If you do not have an analyst available to you, you might wonder whether it is correct for you to work on your dreams or use other techniques of inner work on your own. I believe that you may do so safely and would benefit from learning these methods. There is one proviso: *You must observe the precautions.*

As you read through these chapters you will find some warnings and some suggestions for staying out of trouble. Be sure to take them seriously and follow them. You must understand that when you approach the unconscious you are dealing with one of the most powerful and autonomous forces in human experience. The techniques of inner work are intended to set in motion the great powers of the unconscious, but in a sense this is like taking the cap off a geyser: Things can get out of hand if you are not careful. If you fail to take this process seriously, or try to turn it into mere entertainment, you can hurt yourself.

You need to be particularly careful with Active Imagination. It should not be practiced unless you have someone available who is familiar with this art, someone who knows how to get you back to the ordinary earth if you should be overwhelmed by the inner world. Active Imagination is safe if we obey the rules and use common sense, but it is possible to get in too deep and feel as though we are sinking too far into the unconscious. Your helper can be either an analyst or a layperson who has some experience with Active Imagination. The main point is to have a friend you can call on if you lose your bearings.

None of this should dissuade you from doing inner work. We

are only observing a universal law: Anything that has great power for good can also be destructive if the power is mishandled. If we want to live intimately with the powerful forces of the inner world, we must also respect them.

Alternative Realities:
The World of Dreaming,
the Realm of Imagination

Our verbal patterns betray many of our automatic assumptions: If one discusses a dream with a friend, the friend is likely to ask something like, "Did that detail *really* happen, or only in the dream?" The implication is that what happens in a dream is not "real." In fact, it would be more accurate to ask, "Did it happen in *dream reality*, or in physical reality? In the world of dreaming, or in the ordinary world?"

Both are genuine worlds, both are realities that truly exist. But the world of dreaming, if we only realized it, has more practical and concrete effect on our lives than outer events do. For it is in the world of dreaming that the unconscious is working out its powerful dynamics. It is there that the great forces do battle or combine to produce the attitudes, ideals, beliefs, and compulsions that motivate most of our behavior.

Once we become sensitive to dreams, we discover that every dynamic in a dream is manifesting itself in some way in our practical lives—in our actions, relationships, decisions, automatic routines, urges, and feelings. We believe ourselves to be in conscious control of these elements of life. But this belief is the great illusion of ego-control. These aspects of our lives are actually determined from a far deeper place. It is in the world of *dreaming* that their root sources are revealed in a form that we can see and understand.

Dreams express the unconscious. Dreams are dynamic mosaics, composed of symbols, that express the movements, conflicts, interactions, and developments of the great energy systems within the unconscious.

The unconscious has a particular capacity to create images and to use those images as symbols. It is these symbols that form our dreams, creating a language by which the unconscious communicates its contents to the conscious mind.

Just as a burning fire inherently exudes heat, the unconscious inherently generates symbols. It is simply the nature of the unconscious to do so. As we learn to read those symbols we gain the ability to perceive the workings of the unconscious within us. This ability to produce symbols affects more than just our dreams: All of human life is nourished by the flow of symbolic imagery from the wellsprings in the unconscious:

The symbolic imagery of the unconscious is the creative source of the human spirit in all its realizations. Not only have consciousness and the concepts of its philosophical understanding of the world arisen from the symbol but also religion, rite and cult, art and customs. And because the symbol-forming process of the unconscious is the source of the human spirit, language, whose history is almost identical with the genesis and development of human consciousness, always starts out as a symbolic language. Thus Jung writes: "An archetypal content expresses itself, first and foremost, in metaphors." (Neumann, *Great Mother*, p. 17)

The image-symbols of the unconscious find their way to the level of consciousness mainly by two routes: dreams and imagination. It is easier to grasp the symbolic quality with dreams, for dreams often present mythical creatures and unearthly situations that would be impossible in everyday physical life. People are usually confused by the dream images until they learn that the images are symbolic and are not to be taken literally.

Since dream images make no sense in ordinary terms, people dismiss them as "weird" or meaningless, but actually, dreams are completely coherent. If we take the time to learn their language, we discover that every dream is a masterpiece of symbolic communication. The unconscious speaks in symbols, not to confuse us, but simply because that is its native idiom.

I was never able to agree . . . that the dream is a "facade" behind which its meaning lies hidden—a meaning already known but maliciously, so to speak, withheld from consciousness. To me, dreams are a part of nature, which harbors no intention to deceive, but expresses something as best it can, just as a plant grows or an animal seeks its food as best it can. These forms of life, too, have no wish to deceive our eyes, but we may deceive ourselves because our eyes are shortsighted. Long before I met Freud I regarded the Unconscious, and dreams, which are its direct exponents, as natural processes to which no arbitrariness can be attributed, and above all, no legerdemain. (Jung, *MDR*, p. 161)

We may compare a dream to a screen on which the unconscious projects its inner drama. We see there the various inner personalities that make up much of our total character, the dynamics among the forces that make up the unconscious. These invisible forces and their activities set off charges, so to speak, that are transmitted onto the screen. They take the form of images, and the interplay of the dream images gives us an exact representation of those inner dynamics that go on inside us.

In learning how to understand these images, our conceptual starting point is our realization that they are not to be taken literally: We learn to look for an attitude, an inner personality, an inner development or conflict that clothes itself in the form and color of this image so that it may be *visible* to us in the Land of Dreaming.

IMAGINATION AND SYMBOLS

We have said that dreams are the first of the two great channels of communication from the unconscious; the second is the imagination.

It baffles many people at first to hear that the imagination is an organ of coherent communication, that it employs a highly refined, complex language of symbols to express the contents of the unconscious. Yet, it is true: If we learn to watch it with a practiced eye, we discover that the imagination is a veritable stream of energy and meaningful imagery flowing from the unconscious most of the time.

We may picture two conduits that run from the unconscious to the conscious mind. The first conduit is the faculty of dreaming; the second is the faculty of imagination. Dreaming and imagination have one special quality in common: their power to convert the invisible forms of the unconscious into images that are perceptible to the conscious mind. This is why we sometimes feel as though dreaming is the imagination at work during sleep and the imagination is the dream world flowing through us while we are awake.

Just as the unconscious gives off charges of energy in the night

that create patterns on the screen of the dream-mind, the unconscious also functions during the waking hours. It emits a continual
stream of energetic pulses that find their way to the conscious
mind in the form of feelings, moods, and, most of all, the images
that appear in the imagination. Just as with dreams, the symbolic
meanings of the images may be understood by the person who is
willing to learn.

The material that flows through the imagination takes many
forms, from the frivolous to the visionary. At the bottom of the
scale is the *passive fantasy*: This is the fanciful daydream that flits
across the mind at odd times during the day or sometimes dis-
tracts us for long periods of time. Such fantasies are mere enter-
tainments or distractions that add nothing to consciousness.

At the top of the scale is the *visionary experience*, in which Active
Imagination and religious encounter merge. Active Imagination
is one way of using the imagination constructively to approach the
unconscious; there are many other ways, including profound
forms of meditation.

Our culture in the twentieth century has a tremendous collective prejudice against the imagination. It is reflected in the things
people say: "You are only imagining things," or, "That is only
your fantasy, not reality."

In fact, no one "makes up" anything in the imagination. The
material that appears in the imagination has to originate in the
unconscious. Imagination, properly understood, is a channel
through which this material flows to the conscious mind. To be
even more accurate, imagination is a *transformer* that converts the
invisible material into images the conscious mind can perceive.

The root of the word *imagination* is the Latin word *imago*, meaning "image"; the imagination is the image-forming faculty in the
mind, the organ that has the power to clothe the beings of the
inner world in imagery so that we can see them. The imagination
generates the symbols the unconscious uses to express itself.

A long series of historical and psychological developments over
the centuries have produced our current misunderstandings of
what fantasy and imagination really are. We haven't the space
here to recall all of those developments, but since the prejudice is
so pervasive, it is worth while to look briefly at how fantasy and

imagination were understood by our intellectual ancestors, the ancient Greeks.

Our English word *fantasy* derives from the Greek word *phantasía*. The original meaning of this word is instructive: It meant "a making-visible." It derived from a verb that means "to make visible, to reveal." The correlation is clear: The psychological function of our capacity for fantasy is to *make visible* the otherwise invisible dynamics of the unconscious psyche.

We find here in the psychology of the Greeks a fundamental insight that modern depth psychology has had to rediscover: The human mind is invested with a special power to convert the invisible realm into visible forms so that it can be seen in the mind and contemplated. We call this invisible realm the unconscious: For Plato it was the world of ideal forms; other ancients thought of it as the sphere of the gods, the region of pure spirit. But all sensed one thing: Only our power to *make images* enables us to see it.

For the Greeks, *phantasía* denoted this special faculty in the mind for producing poetic, abstract, and religious imagery. *Phantasía* is our capacity to "make visible" the contents of the inner world by giving them form, by personifying them. The Greeks took for granted the reality of the inner world, expressed as ideal forms or universal qualities that clothed themselves in the divine images of their gods. For them, *phantasía* was the organ by which that divine world spoke to the human mind.*

In European psychology until at least medieval times, the image-forming capacity called imagination or *phantasía* was thought of as the organ that receives meanings from the spiritual and aesthetic worlds and forms them into an inner image that can be held in memory and made the object of thought and reasoning. In religion, the imaginative faculty was the legitimate path of religious inspiration, revelation, and experience. The fact that information entered the conscious mind through the imagination did not in any wise discredit it, for "an experience of poetic imagination

---

*The Romans apparently had no word in Latin for this exact idea of poetic, spiritual, or religious imagination that produced a symbolic representation of inner truth. The word *imaginatio* meant in classical Latin "fictitious," in the sense that the picture is not the same as the external object that it represents. Roman writers came to use the Greek word *phantasía* when they wanted to speak of the human faculty by which we express the contents of the soul by using poetic or spiritual imagery. Cicero used the Greek characters to write the word.

[was] conventionally regarded as accompanied by a belief in the reality of what is imagined (*Oxford English Dictionary*).

It was perhaps in Elizabethan times that the other, parallel meaning of *fantasy* began to take hold—a fictitious daydream, something fanciful and unreal. The word *fancy* was coined—derived from *fantasy*—to mean something that is made up whimsically in the imagination as a mere entertainment. Unfortunately, this is the misunderstanding of the nature of imagination that we have inherited in the popular mind of our century.

If we think about it even briefly, it should be clear how foolish it is to denigrate the imagination. Humans depend on the imagination's image-making power and its image-symbols for poetic imagery, literature, painting, sculpture, and essentially all artistic, philosophical, and religious functioning. We could not develop the abstract intelligence, science, mathematics, logical reasoning, or even language, were it not for our capacity to generate these image-symbols. This is why Neumann could say what was quoted earlier:

> The symbolic imagery of the unconscious is the creative source of the human spirit in all its realizations. . . . And because the symbol-forming process of the unconscious is the source of the human spirit, language, whose history is almost identical with the genesis and development of human consciousness, always starts out as a symbolic language. (Neumann, *Great Mother*, p. 17)

ACTIVE IMAGINATION: THE CONSCIOUS USE OF THE IMAGINATIVE FACULTY

Active Imagination, like the unconscious, has always existed in human life. But as with many facets of our inner life, it took Jung to rediscover the lost art and make it available to modern people.

At first glance, Active Imagination may seem too simple or naive to be taken seriously as a psychological technique: It consists in going to the images that rise up in one's imagination and making a dialogue with them. It involves an encounter with the images. The conscious ego-mind actually enters into the imagination and takes part in it. This often means a spoken conversation with the figures who present themselves, but it also involves entering into the action, the adventure or conflict that is spinning its story out in one's imagination.

It is this awareness, this conscious *participation* in the imaginal event, that transforms it from mere passive fantasy to *Active* Imagination. The coming together of conscious mind and unconscious mind on the common ground of the imaginal plane gives us an opportunity to break down some of the barriers that separate the ego from the unconscious, to set up a genuine flow of communication between the two levels of the psyche, to resolve some of our neurotic conflicts with the unconscious, and thus to learn more about who we are as individuals.

Because of the popular notion that imagination is fictitious, many people react automatically by thinking that such an experience in the imagination would be meaningless. They think, "I would just be talking to myself." But if we work with Active Imagination we soon confirm that we dialogue with genuine interior parts of our own selves. We confront the powerful personalities who live inside us at the unconscious level and who are so often in conflict with our conscious ideas and behavior. We actually enter into the dynamics of the unconscious: We travel into a region where the conscious mind had not known how to go.

This experience, to be sure, is symbolic. The images with whom we interact are symbols, and we encounter them on a symbolic plane of existence. But a magical principle is at work: When we experience the images, *we also directly experience the inner parts of ourselves that are clothed in the images.* This is the power of symbolic experience in the human psyche when it is entered into consciously: Its intensity and its effect on us is often as concrete as a physical experience would be. Its power to realign our attitudes, teach us and change us at deep levels, is much greater than that of external events that we may pass through without noticing.

When we experience the symbol, we simultaneously experience the complex, the archetype, the inner psychic entity that is represented by the symbol. When the image speaks, it is with one of our own inner voices. When we answer back, it is the unseen inner part of our own self that listens and registers. It stands before us in the form of the imaginal image.

In Active Imagination I am not so much "talking to myself" as talking to *one of my selves*. It is in that exchange between the ego and the various characters who rise up from the unconscious and appear in my imagination that I begin to bind the fragmented pieces of myself into a unity. I begin to know, and learn from, the parts of myself I had never known before.

When people ask me if Active Imagination is "real" or if dreams are "real," I always think of a detail in the story of Don Quijote de la Mancha. Don Quijote said he was seeking the "bread that is made from better-than-wheat." He meant, of course, the Host, the bread that is eaten as part of the Christian ritual. The Host is made from wheat, yet it is also fashioned from the archetype, from the body of Christ, from spirit, from better-than-wheat.

In the same figurative sense I can say that Active Imagination is "realer than real." It is not only real in the sense that it has a practical and concrete bearing on our physical lives, it also connects us to a world of forces that are superpersonal and transcendent. It allows us to participate in shaping the flow of the principal streams of energy that join together in each of us to form the long-range patterns of our lives, our relationships, and our attitudes. It affects us on the level of realities that go deeper, and affect us more profoundly, than any local event in our daily lives.

By comparison with these huge inner forces, and the long-range contours and directions that they establish in us, the worries and decisions of daily life turn out to be mostly ripples on the surface of a huge river of life that moves slowly and inexorably toward its goal. Dream work and Active Imagination attune us to the larger vision of life, to the direction of that huge river. They pull our minds briefly off the ripples and local crosscurrents that preoccupy us most of the time.

We therefore come to sense that dream and imagination connect us to a level of existence that is not only "real" in the external sense of reality, it is more than real.

The Archetypes and
the Unconscious

The concept of *archetypes* comes up frequently in dream work or Active Imagination; therefore, it may be helpful to discuss this important concept now, early in our material. Then, as examples of archetypal images appear in our discussion, we will be in a better position to understand their significance. We will look now at the basic ideas contained in the concept of the archetypes; later, as we go through specific dream examples and practical steps, we will have a chance to deepen our understanding of the subject.

The idea of the psychological archetypes is one of Jung's most useful and provocative contributions to modern thought. It has wide application outside the area of psychology and has influenced many scholars working in such areas as anthropology, cultural history, mythology, theology, comparative religion, and literary interpretation. This is because Jung has demonstrated that the archetypes appear in symbolic form, not only in the dreams of individual people, but also in mythology, cultural patterns, religious symbols and rites, and all products of the human imagination, such as literature and art.

The idea of archetypes is an ancient one. It is related to Plato's concept of ideal forms—patterns already existing in the divine mind that determine in what form the material world will come into being. But we owe to Jung the concept of the *psychological* archetypes—the characteristic patterns that pre-exist in the collective psyche of the human race, that repeat themselves eternally in the psyches of individual human beings and determine the basic ways that we perceive and function as psychological beings.

Jung became aware of the existence of the archetypes when he observed that the symbols that arise in people's dreams often correspond exactly to images that have appeared in ancient myths, art, and religion, from times and places of which the dreamer could not possibly have known. He began to sense that there are certain primordial symbols, and certain universal meanings that attach to them in the human unconscious, that spontaneously burst forth from the unconscious in any time or place without needing cultural transmission.

At the same time Jung observed that these "primordial images," as he called them, formed the biological pattern according to which our basic human psychological structure is formed. We might think of them as the natural blueprints that dictate the shape of our inner mental structures, or the basic molds that determine our instinctual roles, values, behavior, creative capacities, and modes of perceiving, feeling, and reasoning.

Because these modes are built-in to the basic collective substratum of the human psyche, they don't have to be transmitted by culture, literature, art, or migration. They arise spontaneously out of the unconscious to appear in the dreams, visions, or imagination of any individual, anywhere, any time. And because they appear as universal, collectively owned images, their symbolism evokes similar feelings, raises similar issues, and constellates similar behavior wherever they arise and enter into the life of an individual or a culture.

The term "archetype" occurs as early as Philo Judaeus, with reference to the *Imago Dei* (God-Image) in man. It can also be found in Irenaeus, who says: "The creator of the world did not fashion these things directly from himself, but copied them from archetypes outside himself." . . . "Archetype" is an explanatory paraphrase of the Platonic [ideal form]. For our purposes this term is apposite and helpful because it tells us that . . . we are dealing with archaic, or—I would say—primordial types, that is, with universal images that have existed since the remotest times. (Jung, 9, *CW*, 5–6)

From the unconscious there emanate determining influences which, independent of tradition, guarantee in every single individual a similarity and even a sameness of experience, and also of the way it is represented imaginatively. One of the main proofs of this is the almost universal parallelism between mythological motifs, which, on account of their quality as primordial images, I have called *archetypes*. (9, *CW*, 118)

We can only suppose that [human] behavior results from patterns of functioning, which I have described as [primordial] *images*. The term "image" is intended to express not only the form of the activity taking place, but the typical situation in which the activity is released. These images are "primordial" images insofar as they are peculiar to whole species, and if they ever "originated" their origin must have coincided at least with the beginning of the species. They are the "human quality" of the human being, the specifically human form his activities take. (9, *CW*, 153)

As the word itself implies, archetypes are related to *types*—types in the sense of a characteristic trait or a set of qualities that seem to appear together over and over again in recognizable, spontaneously recurring patterns. The "virtuous maiden" is a type, the "wise and gentle queen" is a type, the "courageous warrior" is a type, and the "puritan" is a type. Almost no real human being fits exactly any type, for types are, by their very nature, idealized models of character traits or behavior patterns. We find characters in literature and figures in our dreams who exactly fit a type, but real human beings are *combinations* of many types that join together to form one rich, inconsistent, many-faceted human personality.

If we find our way back to the primordial pattern that produced each of these universal *types* that we instinctively recognize as personality traits existing potentially within us all, the primordial image that existed in the mind of the first human as well as in yours and mine, then we will in a sense also find the *original* of the type, the first of the type, the plate from which the page was printed.

The root *arche* in Greek meant "the first," and *type* meant "impress," "imprint," or "pattern." Psychological *archetypes*, then, are the pre-existing "first patterns" that form the basic blueprint for the major dynamic components of the human personality. In a real sense, when we look at the types, we realize that it is they, in combination, that make us identifiably human. They are inborn within us as part of our inheritance as members of the human race.

Not all the images that appear in dreams are archetypes. We should begin by observing that the unconscious is composed of energy, and that it forms itself into distinct energy systems—or what we might call "energy forms." These energy forms can be feelings, attitudes, value systems, or entire personalities that live inside us. Actually, all of us have many distinct personalities coexisting within us at the unconscious level. It is these inner "personalities" that appear to us in our dreams as "persons."

Among these energy forms that present themselves as images in our dreams, there are archetypes. But the greater number are *not* archetypes, do not correspond to universal patterns; they are merely personal energy systems of the dreamer. People often become confused when they first hear of the archetypes and wake up to some of the awesome symbols in which the archetypes appear. They may think that every image that appears in a dream represents an archetype. Or they may get the impression that there is a set list, somewhere, of all the archetypes, and that one could interpret all dream symbols by taking the most likely archetype from the list and applying it to the dream symbol.

Neither of these ideas is accurate. There is probably an infinite number of archetypes, as there are innumerable traits and character patterns that exist universally among humans. Identifying an archetype is a matter of sensing that one is keyed into a universal human energy system, seeing a powerful symbol that springs from deep within our collective human nature; it is not a matter of working from a list of types that someone has made. In this area we have not only the right but the duty to draw on our own creative imagination. We are free to call the archetypes by names that have meaning for us as individuals. Later, we will talk more about this.

Some examples should give a clearer idea of how we encounter archetypes: In all cultures and religions since the beginning of history the idea of the *soul* has sprung up spontaneously. Humankind has always intuited or posited the existence of an entity within that was invisible yet active. Men often referred to their souls as a *feminine* presence in poetry and religious allegory. Sometimes the soul was seen as an inner woman who made a marriage with Christ or made it possible to commune with God. Sometimes men envisioned a feminine muse who inspired them to poetry, literature, art, or refined sensibility. Women, by contrast, often imagined the soul as a masculine presence that provided wisdom and strength.

Jung discovered that what people called the "soul" in religious language actually has a psychological counterpart, a specific and objective part of the inner psyche that acts like the "soul" of religion and poetry and performs the same functions that have been described. In men the soul appears in dreams as a feminine presence. In women, it usually appears as a masculine figure. To distinguish this objective psychological entity from the religious notion, Jung called the feminine figure the *anima* and called the masculine figure in women's dreams the *animus*. These two words mean "soul" and "spirit," respectively, in Latin.

In later chapters we will see some examples of the appearance of anima and animus in dreams and imagination. The point here is that the main characteristic of an archetype is its universality, that it produces a structure or an energy form that appears to exist in the psychological structures of all men and women, everywhere. This is true of the soul, both as an objective entity and as a universal symbol. These are part of our human heritage, part of what makes us human.

Not only does the soul exist among all people as an inner reality, but it generates a universal set of symbols—the various images of anima and animus—by which it represents itself. So we can find a similar set of images in the dreams of most men for the anima, as well as in myth, folktales, religion, art, and literature. And the same is true of the universal symbolism of the animus for women.

Just as an archetype may be most easily identified as an inner *structure*, as in the case of anima and animus, it may also be a universal *quality* that all people recognize or a universal way of feeling and behaving that we all pass through. For example, a woman might dream that she found herself in the presence of the god or goddess of love. Love is an archetype: To love is a preformed tendency in humans, part of the primordial blueprint for our human way of feeling, relating, and acting toward others. It finds its way into every person and every culture. It is so universal that to say so seems unnecessary.

The woman who dreams of this archetype is not made up only of the urge to love. She also has the capacity for hatred or spite, as we all do, hidden away somewhere within her total personality. But in her dream she is in the presence of an image that represents the *archetype* of love—love as a universal, superpersonal force that rushes out of some place deep in the primordial psyche of our species.

In the face of that image, if she can see that it is the universal energy of love that is challenging her and affecting her, she can better understand her feelings, emotions, and behavior.

We mentioned earlier that there are innumerable archetypes in the human unconscious. Determining that one is dealing with an archetype in one's dream is a matter of sensing when some universal human instinct or pattern is behind the image—or recognizing a symbol as one of those primordial images that bespeak the timeless and ubiquitous human qualities.

We don't need to know which of these have been officially designated as archetypes by Jung. We don't need to know by what names Jungians have called them, although that might be helpful at times.

Jungians usually find their names for the archetypes in myths and ancient religions, because that is where the images first appeared, often in their most dramatic and memorable form. For example, the archetype of the heroic journey in which one is tested by fate is often called an "odyssey" because its greatest image is the journey of Odysseus. But all such names are to some extent arbitrary. We are all free to use our own judgment, feelings, and imagination in deciding whether we are dealing with an archetype, and we are free to use the names for them that are most meaningful to us.

Years ago a young graduate student came to work on his dreams with me, and a masculine figure began to appear repeatedly in his dreams. The student spontaneously invented his own name for this friendly male companion that showed a universal character. He called him "the tribal brother."

The dreamer and his tribal brother lived among a tribe of Vikings in an ancient age in Europe. In some dreams he and his companion were warriors and went to battle together. In others, they were healers. In one they discovered a radiant and magical woman in a white robe who became the dreamer's consort. Together, they went through all the struggles and numinous discoveries of young manhood. The dreamer's friendship with his inner figure was so close, and felt so real, that he felt lonely whenever he had to go for many days without seeing him in his dreams.

It is apparent that the "tribal brother" is an archetype, and that there is a corresponding "tribal sister" archetype in the structures of women. Men and women often dream of such a figure in the years of early adulthood—someone of the same age and sex who is their help, their loyal ally, and their companion in the trials and challenges of life. And the image corresponds to an objective reality, for the energy system actually lives inside the individual and lends its strength and consciousness to his or her development, just as the image describes. In a woman, the tribal sister is an archetype of feminine consciousness that augments her sense of her feminine side and fortifies her identity as she evolves into mature womanhood.

I cite this example to emphasize that you have the right to make your own judgments and choose your own names. No one will find "tribal brother" written in some standard list of archetypes or a dictionary of symbols. Nevertheless, a dreamer saw this symbol in his dream, recognized it as a universal image in human life, and found a name for it that comes out of the archaic past. This is within your power as well as his.

It sometimes makes it easier to see how the personalities who appear in our dreams correspond to great forces in human nature if we compare the archetypes to the ancient Greeks' conception of the gods. The gods, as the Greeks conceived them, were *forces* that interacted with individual human lives. These forces were present in every life, yet were universal, timeless, and lived outside the limits of a particular life or time. "The gods" could as well have been described as "fields of energy" acting on the human race. Yet their images presented *integrated personalities* that are similar to the "persons" in our dreams who carry an aura of great power and fit some great type in human nature.

For this reason Jung said that the heroes and gods of the Greek pantheon were actually symbols par excellence for the archetypes. Their images express the universal, primordial types that make up the human personality.

Strictly speaking, the archetypes are not forces, but rather the pre-existing patterns that give typical shape to the forces in us. Nevertheless, when we encounter the images of the archetypes we always feel the power that has been shaped by the image. We feel that we have tapped into not only a symbolic type but also a huge reservoir of superhuman power in the collective human unconscious. We can feel the archetype as a charge of energy. It feels as though it were outside us, something the conscious mind has to interact with, deal with. When we see them at work as forces that move us and influence us, we can begin to understand why the

Greeks and other ancient peoples understood or experienced them as supernatural powers.

Because the energy systems formed by the archetypes are transpersonal, universal, corresponding to timeless and primordial realities, we actually experience the archetypes in dreams as though they were divinities or gods. We experience them as the Great Powers. They sometimes help us, sometimes threaten us, alternately strengthen or overwhelm us, liberate us or possess us, depending on the evolution we are passing through and the issues involved. We feel them as great, transcendent, eternal energies that are outside our control even as they are part of our lives and nature.

As with most psychological concepts, there is much in the idea of the archetypes that is connected to ordinary, everyday life. We feel and sense the archetypes at work in our daily lives without identifying them as such.

For example, if we know a woman who has struggled against overwhelming odds and shown superhuman courage, we will say, "She is a heroine. She has performed heroically through all this." Without thinking about it, we acknowledge that the archetype of the heroine lives in her, forms part of her character, and that she has behaved in accord with that universal type that we instinctively know.

In another case we may say that a man we know "acts like a Scrooge." We mean that the archetype of the cynical miser—another type or personality pattern we all recognize—manifests in that man's attitudes and behavior.

The archetype of the hero or heroine lives in each of us. So does the archetype of the miser. This is why we instantly recognize them in others. In some people a particular archetype is strongly in evidence: We can see it "written all over them." In others, the archetypes are potentialities that remain in the unconscious. The heroic archetype, for example, may surface in a particular person only when a crisis demands it, or love or loyalty inspire it.

None of us is just one thing. We are not monodimensional creatures; we are rich combinations of the infinitely varied archetypes. Each of us is part heroine or hero and part coward, part parent and part child, part saint and part thief. It is in learning to identify these great archetypal motifs within ourselves, learning to honor each one as a legitimate human trait, learning to live out the energy of each in a constructive way, that we make inner work a great odyssey of the spirit.

The archetypes are often presented by the unconscious in images that are divine, royal, magical, or mythical. If the archetype of the universal heroine appears in your dream, she may take on the visage of a legendary figure like Joan of Arc. She may have on shining armor or carry a magical sword. Generally there will be something that creates the feeling of nobility or authority.

Even if the specific feeling of awe, divinity, or magic is not present, there may be a feeling that one is looking at the prototypical example of the universal type, quality, or experience: the Mother of Mothers, Father Time, the war that is Armageddon, the love that encompasses all human experience of love that has ever been.

Conflict and Unification:
Credo In Unum

Because inner work is a dialogue between conscious and unconscious elements, it always raises the specter of conflict—inner conflict over values, urges, beliefs, ways of life, morals, loyalties. The conflicts, of course, are there in any case, regardless of whether we face up to them. But our dream work forces us to look at them. And Active Imagination, perhaps more than any other form of inner work, brings the conflicts to the surface and gets them out in the open.

How can we stand to bring them into the open? Most people can't face inner conflict at all; they impose a kind of artificial unity on life by clinging to the prejudices of their ego and repressing the voices of the unconscious. If there are other parts of ourselves who have different values or different needs, most of us would rather not hear about it.

We have already talked about the pluralism of our inner structure. We know that, although we seem to be individuals, we are actually *plural* beings. Each of us has a great multitude of distinct personalities coexisting within one body, sharing one psyche. We also know that the human mind experiences the world as a duality: We divide the world and our own selves into darkness and light, "good" and "bad," and we stand eternally in judgment, siding first with one side, then with the other, but rarely undertaking the terrible task of integrating all this into a whole.

It is perhaps this human tendency to see everything as "good" or "bad" that creates the greatest obstacle to accepting and utilizing our varied inner personalities. We don't realize that our categories of "good" and "bad" are usually arbitrary and subjective. We derive most of these standards from family, culture, and childhood conditioning without questioning them. If we have the courage to look with open minds at some of the instincts and energy systems within that we have been so ashamed of, we almost always find that they can also be positive strengths—and that they are merely normal parts of a total human character. As with all our inner contents, they need to be acknowledged, honored, and lived on an appropriate and constructive level.

It takes courage to go to the "bad" side of ourselves, to acknowledge it as part of ourselves, to consider that it could have a constructive role to play in our lives. It takes courage to look directly at the fragmentation of our desires and urges. One side seems to argue yes while another side vehemently says no. One side of my psyche argues for relatedness, rootedness, and stability. Another side wants to go on heroic crusades, have great adventures in exotic places, travel to the other side of the world and live like a gypsy. Yet another personality wants to build an empire and consolidate my power systems. Sometimes these conflicts seem irreconcilable, and we feel torn apart in the conflicts of desires, duties, and obligations that we feel.

How, then, can we go to the unconscious in our inner work and immerse ourselves in this fragmentation and duality? We could not find the courage to face up to the terrible divisions in us unless we felt instinctively that the conflicts must eventually resolve, the warring parts come together in peace, the fragmentation finally reveal a deeper reality, an underlying fundamental unity and meaning in life.

A good place to begin our understanding of inner work—although it may seem strange to you at first—is with the Credo, the Nicene Creed. *Credo In Unum Deum*: I believe in One God.

Millions of people repeat this statement in one language or another every week. Of course, most of us never consider its implications; it has become another phrase to repeat without thinking about it. Whatever may be your feeling about the creed as a literal, religious statement, you should consider what it means on a psychological level. It says that there is only one subject; there is only one Source, one beginning, one unity out of which all the multiplicity of this life flows, and to which it returns.

Because we sense this principle, we know that no matter what conflicts we encounter, no matter what tangles and collisions we find within ourselves, they are all branches from one trunk.

Without this conviction we would be helpless; serious dream work and the confrontations of Active Imagination would be impossible. The sheer multiplicity of our inner selves would over-whelm us. But the Credo teaches us that all these selves, all these energies, flow from one indivisible source and can be traced back to that One. One way of doing that tracing is to enter bravely into the pluralism, into the duality, through inner work.

Who isn't plagued most of a lifetime by this duality of life? Mas-culine and feminine voices within, duty or desire, good or evil, this choice or that choice, follow my heart or follow my mind—we can go on forever reciting the pairs of opposites that express the *yin* and *yang* of life.

Since we will use these terms *yin* and *yang* again, it may help to explain what is meant. In ancient Chinese psychology and philos-ophy these words denoted the inherent spontaneous division of the world into pairs of opposites: darkness and light, hot and cold, masculine and feminine. The early sages taught that a grasp of total reality required keeping the pairs of opposites in balance.

Yang denoted masculine, in motion, activist, hard, warm, dry, light. *Yin* denoted feminine, at rest, receptive, soft, cold, dark. The sense in which we use the terms in Jungian psychology is as an expression for the general human psychological experience of duality. We always contain within us attitudes that are comple-mentary opposites. Part of us is in favor, part of us is opposed. Part of us wants to move ahead, part of us wants to be quiet and see how things go. One attitude comes from the feminine side, another from the masculine.

Wisdom, according to the ancient sages, comes from letting the *yin* side predominate when its time comes and functioning from the *yang* side when its turn comes. Regardless of the subject, balance comes only when both sides are given their due.

But without this duality, this division of the cosmos, there could be no human life as we know it. It is the price that is paid for our incarnation as conscious beings who inevitably learn to divide the world and to see ourselves as distinct from it.

The path toward consciousness begins when we learn to break the primordial unity of our original unconsciousness. Like Adam in the Garden of Eden, we learn to see ourselves as distinct from the world and the people around us. We learn to divide the world into categories, to classify. We begin to divide not only the phe-nomena outside us but our own traits and characteristics into opposites: what seems "good" from what seems "bad," the things that frighten us from the things that comfort us, that which affirms us from that which threatens and humiliates us. Thus we arrive at self-consciousness, a sense of ourselves as individuals who stand apart from the herd, egos who stand apart from the collective unconscious.

But the price that is paid for this consciousness is a heavy one: the fragmentation, the seemingly irreconcilable conflicts within us, the feeling that the universe has fallen apart and has no central core of meaning. We are conscious enough to be torn by the conflicts of life but not yet conscious enough to sense life's underlying unity. Yet, it is by this path that Nature becomes aware of its own existence by giving birth to its one witness: human consciousness.

"But why on earth," you may ask, "should it be necessary for man to achieve, by hook or by crook, a higher level of consciousness?" This is truly the crucial question, and I do not find the answer easy. Instead of a real answer I can only make a confession of faith: I believe that, after thousands and millions of years, someone had to realize that this wonderful world of mountains and oceans, suns and moons, galaxies and nebulae, plants and animals, *exists*. From a low hill in the plains of East Africa I once watched the vast herds of wild animals grazing in soundless stillness, as they had done from time immemorial, touched only by the breath of a primeval world. I felt then as if I were the first man, the first creature, to know that all this *is*. The entire world around me was still in a primeval state; it did not know that it *was*. And then, in that one moment in which I came to know, the world sprang into being; without that moment it would never have been. All Nature seeks this goal and finds it fulfilled in man. . . . Every advance, even the smallest, along this path of conscious realization adds that much to the world. (Jung, 9, I, *CW* par. 177)

Once we have stood apart, once we have brought the world into being by becoming conscious of it as distinct from ourselves, our task is still not finished. Each of us carries an intuition, a latent conviction that all this finally adds up to a meaning. There is a universal sense in humans that there is unity and cohesion at the heart of life, and that it is possible for us to be consciously aware of it. So far as I can discover, it is this awareness of the primordial and essential unity of the human psyche that most religions and philosophies have referred to as *enlightenment*.

Inner work teaches us one of the most important principles of the path toward the unified self. Many people believe they can achieve unity by going backwards, avoiding the conflicts, pretending they aren't there. Inner work, as a practical experience, shows us that we can *embrace* the conflict, embrace the duality, bravely place ourselves in the very midst of the warring voices, and find our way *through* them to the unity that they ultimately express.

We cannot go backwards. We can't retreat. We can't find our primordial sense of unity by canceling out consciousness and retreating to animal unconsciousness. Our evolution has taken a different path, and that path is built into us as surely as is the structure of our physical bodies. Our path leads straight ahead, not around the duality but through it to a consciousness of its underlying oneness. Our task is to find the fundamental unity and meaning of life without sacrificing our consciousness of our pluralism, our sense of ourselves as distinct and individual beings.

It is because the cosmos gets divided into heaven and earth, and because heaven and earth are in dialogue, that the universe has produced a Christ, a Buddha, a Mohammed, and the prophets. Each of them carries the archetype of the unified self and the message that the many are actually one. It is because of the conflicts in our own personal lives—and our willingness to face them and convert them into constructive dialogue—that we grow toward consciousness.

It is our lot, if we are honest, to live in duality and paradox. The dialogue of those paradoxical elements is the stuff of life. Surprisingly it is also the surest path toward unity. Our dreams are its stage, its workshop and battleground. And Active Imagination is its superb language.

II. DREAM WORK

Approaching Dream Work

Since this book is intended to give a direct, practical approach to dream work, we will not spend much time talking about theories. However, there are some concepts and terms used in Jungian dream analysis that are very useful for orienting us to the world of dreams. Since they will come up from time to time, we will take the opportunity to discuss them now. Then we will go through the practical steps in order to learn how to use them.

A good starting point is to look at an actual dream, which we can then use to illustrate some of the basic ideas. This is the dream of a young professional woman who leads a very busy life. The dream is short and simple, on the surface, but it had a powerful impact on the dreamer.

The Renegade Dream

I am looking for my car keys. I realize my husband has them. Then I remember that my brother has borrowed my car and has not returned it. I see both of them and I call to them. They do not seem to hear me. Then a disheveled young man, like a "renegade," gets into my car and drives off. I feel extremely frustrated, helpless, and somewhat abandoned.

For her work on this dream, the dreamer began with two basic principles: First, the basic function of dreams is to express the unconscious. She realized, therefore, that the dream was expressing something that existed within her at the unconscious level. Second, she knew that the images in the dream should not be taken literally but as symbols of parts of herself and dynamics within her inner life. She did both dream work and Active Imagination with the characters in her dream. This was the basic interpretation that resulted:

Because of the spontaneous associations she made in her mind with her husband and brother, she felt that they represented the part of herself that needed to be quiet, meditative, and centered within herself. She saw that she was so busy with her extroverted professional life that she had no time for home, family, and the quiet time that kept her centered. She had been taking on more than she could handle, teaching classes as well as carrying a big work load. She was overworked, edgy, unable to find time to be alone or to be with her husband. She said yes to every request, agreed to join in every project.

The car represented to her this overinvolvement. That pattern felt like a "vehicle" that she entered and that ran away with her. Like the car, the pattern was mechanical, a product of collective society, and somehow out of her control. She felt as though something had pushed her into the car, turned the switch, and "drove away" with her into another project, another involvement.

She associated the other masculine figure, the "renegade" who drove the car away, with the part of herself that always wanted to be in high gear, that was saying yes to everything, that loved to turn on the ignition and charge off in the collective circles. He was like a wild person who couldn't stand to sit still or be quiet. The dreamer felt split between the side of life represented by her husband and brother and the side represented by the renegade.

In response to this dream, she made some drastic changes in her schedule. She cut down her involvements in the world outside, gave herself more time to be with her family, be quiet, and do inner work. There was an immediate sense of relief as her energy was focused on the aspects of life that were most important to her.

This dream illustrates several basic principles that will help us. First, an important point: Even a short, seemingly insignificant dream tries to tell us something that we need to know. Dreams never waste our time. If we take the trouble to listen to the "little" dreams, we find that they carry important messages.

Who are these characters who populate our dreams? What is it in our inner structure that is represented by figures like the husband, the brother, the renegade? For this woman, we have seen that the husband's image represented something distinct from her literal, physical husband—something within her own inner being. In this dream, his image represented a *life-principle* at work within her, a set of values, an inner sense of what way of life was most true to her essential character.

The multiplicity of dream figures reflects the plurality and multidimensional structure of the inner self. We are all made up of many personalities or inner "persons," coexisting within one mind and one body. We think of ourselves as one individual, with one single viewpoint on life, but actually, if we pay attention, we have to admit that it feels as though there were several people living somewhere deep inside, each pulling in a different direction.

Dreams show us, in symbolic form, all the different personalities that interact within us and make up our total self. In the Renegade Dream, the dreamer found several aspects of herself represented by the images of husband, brother, and renegade. One part of her wants to stay at home, tend the garden, meditate, and enjoy her family. One part wants to do good work in her profession. Another part of her wants to go out and save the world, charge off with the "renegade" into endless crusades and "good works." The "renegade" part of her, in fact, seems to be a slightly disheveled manifestation of the archetypal *hero* living within her. By showing her all this, the dream makes it clear she must find a balance among all these opposing urges and values.

Jung observed that each of our psychological components is a distinct center of consciousness. We can think of them as structures within ourselves that make up our total psyche. We can see them as independent energy systems that combine in us, for they are *autonomous*: Each has its own consciousness, its own values, desires, and points of view. Each leads us in a different direction; each has a different strength or quality to contribute to our lives; and each has its own role in our total character.

This is why they often feel as though they were independent *people* living on the inside. It is appropriate that they are symbolized as *persons* in our dreams.

Often when we think that we are trying to make a decision based on facts or logic, we are actually caught in a battle between terrible forces inside us. Since it is mostly unconscious, and we don't know who fights for what, we can't make peace. We don't know which side to take. We feel ourselves hopelessly split between opposing forces.

Here is a woman in a novel by a contemporary writer, divided within as she faces her seducer:

"Then we can travel together," he explained, as if this were the solution both of them had been working towards.

She said nothing at all. Inside her it was as if each component of her nature had gone to war against the other: the child fought the mother, the tart fought the nun . . .

(LeCarre, *Little Drummer Girl*, p. 78)

Who is this child who fights the mother, this tart who fights the nun? What of the man whose inner hero wants to storm castles and quest for the Holy Grail while his inner monk wants to stay quiet in his cell and contemplate the divine mystery? We might say that these represent human possibilities, aspects of human character that are common to us all.

Here we encounter the *archetypes*: the universal patterns or tendencies in the human unconscious that find their way into our individual psyches and form us. They are actually the psychological building blocks of energy that combine together to create the individual psyche. Here are the type of the child, the type of the mother, the universal virgin, and the universal tart, all flowing through the personality of one individual.

In our dreams, they join the archetypal hero or heroine, the priest, the scoundrel. Each of them adds a different richness to our character and has a different truth to tell. Each represents our own, individual version of the universal forces that combine to create a human life.

The inner self is not only plural: Jung found that the psyche manifests itself as an *androgyny*, containing both feminine and masculine energies. Every man needs to connect the "masculine" ego to the side of his psyche that the unconscious sees as his "feminine" side. Each woman's feminine ego needs to make a synthesis with the symbolically "masculine" side of her total self.

The psyche spontaneously divides itself into pairs of opposites. All the archetypal energies in us appear to the conscious mind as complementary pairs: *yin* and *yang*, feminine and masculine, dark and light, positive and negative. Part of me lives in the conscious mind, and part of me—the complementary quality that completes the whole—is hidden in the unconscious. The unconscious constantly uses the masculine-feminine dichotomy to symbolize the interplay of the inner forces that must balance and complete one another. They may appear as hostile opposites, deadly enemies, yet they are destined to make a synthesis, for they are two facets of one stream of energy.

Figures of the opposite sex often appear in dreams to symbolize the energy systems that are the farthest from the ego, farthest from the conscious mind, deep in the unconscious of the dreamer. It is impossible to predict for a particular woman or man what inner parts will be represented by an image of the opposite sex. It depends on the individual, but some common patterns are clear and useful to know.

Men have been traditionally conditioned in our culture to identify with the thinking and organizing side of life, to be heroes and doers. The unconscious often chooses a feminine figure, therefore, to represent a man's emotional nature, his capacity for feeling, appreciating beauty, developing values, and relating through love. These are the capacities that in many men live mostly in the unconscious. Their appearance in a man's dream in feminine imagery signals his need to make them conscious, expand the narrow focus of his "masculine" ego-life.

The ego structure of many women is identified mostly with feeling, relatedness, nurturing, and mothering—qualities that are traditionally thought of as "feminine." The feminine side of the psyche is also rational, but it uses feeling-logic, the rational processes that are based on feeling, on sensing fine differentiations of values. It "knows" by a different mode than does the masculine side—by sensing the *whole* rather than by analyzing. Women's dreams therefore often use masculine figures to represent the other side of the psyche—thinking-logic, knowing by analyzing and differentiating, classifying, organizing, competing, wielding power. A woman may find that many of her attitude principles, such as her ideas about religion, philosophy, and politics, will be generated from the side of her psyche that is represented by masculine figures.

The most important aspect of the androgynous psyche is the *soul-image*. In every man and woman there is an inner being whose primary function in the psyche is to serve as the *psychopomp*—the one who guides the ego to the inner world, who serves as mediator between the unconscious and the ego.

Jung became aware of the soul-image when he sensed a feminine presence within himself who pulled him toward the unconscious, who embodied the part of himself that lived in the realm of dream and imagination. When she appeared in his dreams, he found she was a creature of mythical quality, seemingly magical and half-divine. Like Beatrice, in the *Divine Comedy* of Dante, she led him to the inner world of the unconscious and served as his guide there. He found the same archetypal feminine presence in other men. He also observed a corresponding masculine soul-image in the dreams and lives of women.

Jung felt that this inner person corresponds to the traditional religious conception of the soul as an inner part of ourselves that connects us to the spiritual realm and leads us to God, so he referred to the feminine soul-image in men as *anima* and to the masculine soul-image in women as *animus*. *Anima* and *animus* are Latin words for *soul*.

It is important to be aware of the soul-images. They appear regularly in our dreams and play a tremendous role in our development as individuals. They affect the entire course of our lives.

Both as energies within us and as powerful symbols, the soul-images are tremendous forces to be reckoned with. All our inborn desire for unity and meaning, our desire to bring the opposing parts of ourselves together, to go to the unconscious and explore the inner world, to find religious experience, is concentrated in these inner beings who are the mediators between our egos and the vast unconscious. If we don't interact with the anima or animus in our inner work, we inevitably project them into areas of our lives where they don't belong.

For example, a man may project his anima into his job and become obsessive with it, making his work into an inferior channel for his religious life. A woman may project her animus onto an external man and fall in love not so much with the human being but with the soul-image that she has projected onto him. The whole basis of the romantic fantasy that so often sabotages ordinary human love is the projection of a man's anima onto a woman or a woman's animus onto an external man. In this way people try to complete themselves through another human being, try to live out the unconscious, unrealized parts of themselves through the external person on whom they put the romantic projection.

In the introduction I spoke of the process of individuation. As you know, individuation is a movement toward consciousness of the total inner self. Using our dreams as models, we can see that individuation also consists to a great extent in bringing the different inner persons within us together in a synthesis. Individuation is not only becoming conscious of these inner energy systems, it is also bringing relatedness and unity among them.

The end product of this evolution is something we can sense, feel, and describe intuitively even though we have not yet attained it—the sense of wholeness, of being completed. The wholeness of our total being, and our consciousness of the quality of wholeness, is expressed in an archetype. Jung called this archetype the *self*.

The self is the principle of integration. It is also the whole—the entire person. When a symbol of the self appears in a dream, it represents not only the totality of our being, but also our potential capacity for the highest consciousness—the awareness of unity in ourselves and in the cosmos.

Dreams constantly record the process of individuation and the movement of the ego toward the self. In most dreams we see an immediate, local situation in our lives. But, at the same time, if you collect your dreams together and see them in the aggregate, they report the stages along the way in the journey toward the self.

The self has characteristic symbols: The circle, the mandala (a circle divided into four parts), the square, and the diamond are all abstract figures that express the archetypal self.

The self is present in all quaternity dreams—dreams involving four characters or in some way emphasizing the number four. Jung found that numbers are archetypal symbols. The number four has been used in every religion from ancient times to the present to symbolize the wholeness of the cosmos or the completion of a spiritual evolution.

Another characteristic symbol of the self is the divine or royal couple: The conjunction of the polarities of masculine and feminine, like the conjunction of the dragons Yin and Yang, symbolizes the highest synthesis of the self.

There is yet one other basic energy system in the unconscious that appears regularly in our dreams and is useful to know about. Jung called this inner being the *shadow*. In every person there is a part of the unconscious that is very close to the ego and usually appears as the same gender as the dreamer. The shadow is a kind of alter ego, split off from the conscious ego-mind and sentenced to live in the unconscious. Usually the shadow contains qualities and traits, both negative and positive, that are a natural part of the ego-personality. But the ego, for one reason or another, has either failed to assimilate these qualities or has repressed them outright. Sometimes the qualities in the shadow seem embarrassing or primitive to the ego: One doesn't want to admit that they belong to one. Sometimes the shadow has tremendous positive strengths that the ego won't claim because it would mean either too much responsibility or a shattering alteration of one's puny self-image.

How the shadow appears in a dream depends on the ego's attitude. For example, if a man's attitude is friendly toward his inner shadow, and he is willing to grow and change, the shadow will often appear as a helpful friend, a "buddy," a tribal brother who helps him in his adventures, backs him up, and teaches him skills. If he is trying to repress his shadow, it will usually appear as a hateful enemy, a brute or monster who attacks him in his dreams. The same principles apply to a woman. Depending on her relationship to her shadow, she may appear as a loving sister or as a frightful witch.

These are some of the basic concepts and models in Jungian dream work that most people find useful when first approaching dreams. They will become more clear as we work with sample dreams and learn the practical steps in the chapters ahead.

The Four-Step Approach

Before we begin step one it may help to have a brief preview of the four basic steps we will be covering in the pages ahead. The steps are these:

1. Making associations
2. Connecting dream images to inner dynamics
3. Interpreting
4. Doing rituals to make the dream concrete

In the first step we form the foundation for interpreting the dream by finding the associations that spring out of our unconscious in response to the dream images. Every dream is made up of a series of images, so our work begins with discovering the meanings that those images have.

In the second step, we look for and find the parts of our inner selves that the dream images represent. We find the dynamics at work inside us that are symbolized by the dream situation. Then, in the third step, the interpretation, we put together the information we have gleaned in the first two steps and arrive at a view of the dream's meaning when taken as a whole.

At the fourth step we learn to do rituals that will make the dream more conscious, imprint its meaning more clearly on our minds, and give it the concreteness of immediate physical experience. When we arrive at the fourth step, we will discuss the uses that ceremony and ritual can have for us in reconnecting with the unconscious.

With this brief road map before us, we will start now with the first step.

Step One: Associations

For every symbol in a dream the unconscious is ready to provide the associations that explain the symbol's meaning. The unconscious contains within itself the references for every symbol that it generates; therefore, the symbolic language of the unconscious can be decoded. Our task begins with waking up to the associations that spontaneously flow out of us in response to symbols.

First, go through your dream and write out every association that you have with each dream image. A dream may contain persons, objects, situations, colors, sounds, or speech. Each of these, for our purposes, is a distinct *image* and needs to be looked at in its own right.

The basic technique is this: Write down the first image that appears in the dream. Then ask yourself, "What feeling do I have about this image? What words or ideas come to mind when I look at it?" Your *association* is any word, idea, mental picture, feeling, or memory that pops into your mind when you look at the image in the dream. It is literally *anything* that you spontaneously connect with the image.

Usually every image will inspire several associations. Each brings to mind a certain person, word, phrase, or memory. Write down each association that comes directly from the image. Then go back to the image and see what other associations come to mind. Keep returning to the dream image and writing down each association that is produced in your mind. Only after you have written all the associations that you find in that one image should you go on to the next image and begin the same process.

At first, this may feel like a lot of work. But after you do it a few times and discover the amazing power of this technique to key you into the meaning of your dream symbols, you will feel that it is well worth the effort. You will also begin to see why symbols have such power over human beings: Symbols connect us spontaneously to the deep parts of ourselves that we have longed to touch.

At this point you should not try to decide which association is the so-called right one. Often the first connection that comes up, the one that seems so obvious, is not the one that will work best for you later on in the process. The unconscious doesn't follow the pathways of ego-logic. An association that feels silly, off-the-wall, irrational, may turn out to be the one that makes the most sense after you work awhile. Sometimes *all* the associations turn out to be relevant to your dream, although they seem contradictory at first. So don't try to choose among them at this point. Just write them down.

Suppose you have a dream that begins: "I am in a blue room." The first image you have to work with is the color blue. These might be the associations you would produce:

Blue: Sad or depressed—"blue mood," "I've got the blues."

Blue moon.

Color of clarity: cool, detached consciousness contrasted with lively, emotional red.

My blue sweater. I usually wear blue.

My grandmother's living room. Always blue.

Blew—"blown away."

"True blue"—means honest and faithful.

It is no accident that the unconscious produces the color blue in one scene, but uses red in another or black in yet another. Blue is used because this particular color expresses the dynamic at work in the unconscious. The meaning that blue has for the unconscious will be found somewhere in the associations to this color that the unconscious produces.

Depending on who the dreamer is, the color could represent clarity and detached contemplation. This use of the symbol might, when interpreted in step three, turn out to mean that a person who is completely controlled by feelings needs to be a little more cool and clear. For another person, the color blue could turn out to be a comment that things are *too* cool, too abstract, without enough redblooded human energy or Dionysian feeling.

For one person, the blue room could represent a depressed feeling: the dream here would refer to the colloquial expression "I feel blue" or "I've got the blues." Your own association could be to your general reaction to that color: "I feel quiet and peaceful when there are blue things around me."

It does not matter how farfetched the association seems to you. This is the stage of dream work in which you simply gather information from the unconscious. You are, in effect, asking the unconscious, "What are the meanings that *you* associate with *your own* symbol?"

Many different reactions will come out of each person. The purpose is to find out what your own unique associations are, not what someone else tells you they *ought* to be according to some book or some theory of psychology. So don't be embarrassed by your associations; don't censor them; don't try to make them sound more elegant or "proper." Just take them as they come.

MAKING DIRECT ASSOCIATIONS

Each time you make a connection, be sure to return to the original dream image. Make a new association from the original image. Always go back to the dream image and start over again from there. Don't make chain associations.

Chain associations are when we make connections with the *associations* rather than with the original dream image. (This is also called "free association.") You make your first association, then you make another association to that one, and then another association to that one, until you have a whole chain. If we do this we never get back to the original dream image.

An example of chain associating would be this:

BLUE → Sad → Hospital → Aunt Jennie → Apple pie → Warm kitchen

You can see that this chain leads farther and farther away from the original image, the color blue. By the time we get to "hospital" or "Aunt Jennie" we have already lost any direct connection to the color blue.

The correct method can be pictured as a wheel, with the dream image at the hub, and the associations radiating out like spokes from the center. All associations proceed from the original image. We always return to the center of the wheel before we go to the next association. One woman I know does all her dream analysis this way, diagraming each image as the center of a wheel:

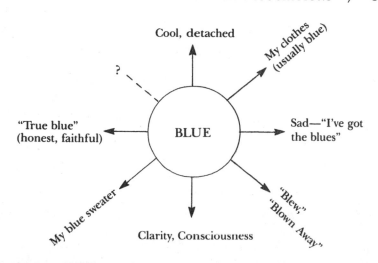

BEING SENSITIVE TO COLLOQUIALISMS

Many of the associations that come up spontaneously are collo-quialisms. The unconscious often uses symbols that bring up col-loquial phrases like "I've got the blues." This is because our collo-quial expressions come out of olden times, when our language was richer in concrete imagery and closer to the archetypes. They come out of the simple, down-to-earth everyday life; therefore, they are excellent language for the unconscious.

A common example is the dream motif of flying. If you find yourself flying in a dream, it can bring to mind a wealth of collo-quial expressions: "I'm flying high." "My head's in the clouds." "I should be more down-to-earth."

These colorful phrases all express a condition that we call *infla-tion*. The ego gets inflated when we are caught up in a power sys-tem, when we are lost in an ideal or abstraction at the expense of ordinary humanness, when the ego has been puffed up by identi-fying with an archetype and has lost all sense of its limits. Then we start "flying high," and the cure is to "get our feet back on the ground."

Similarly, when a dream says that someone is "blowing smoke" or is "full of hot air," we immediately have a sense of what the dream is trying to say. If there is a jewel in your dream, you may ask in what respect the dream is saying that you "are a jewel." On the other hand, if a dream says, "He is a jackass," we may also ponder how *that* applies to us!

USING THE "IT CLICKS" METHOD

This leads us to the question of how we are to choose one of these associations. Which one is going to lead me to a correct interpretation?

Jung had an answer that sounds deceptively simple: He said that one of the associations will "click"! As you go through your associations, one of them will generate a lot of energy in you. You will see how it fits together with other symbols in the dream. Or you may feel a spot touched in you where you are wounded and confused. You may find that this association makes you see something in yourself that you had never looked at before. In that moment, you will get a rush of conviction from somewhere deep inside: *It fits. It clicks.*

Although this method sounds too simple, it is reliable. Remember that dreams are created out of energy. One way to find the essence of a dream symbol is to *go where the energy is*—go to the association that brings up a surge of energy. Every symbol is calculated to rouse us, to wake us up. It is organically tied to energy systems deep in the substrata of the unconscious. When you make a connection that is very close to the energy source, sparks fly. It is as though you had touched a live wire. You feel intuitively that you have tapped into the energy behind your dream: The association *clicks*.

Sometimes it is not clear at first which association is most accurate or more useful for understanding your dream. In that case it is better to leave it alone for a while and go on to the next symbol. Don't lock yourself into one meaning for the symbol; keep an open mind until you begin to tie the whole dream together. Let your understanding of the symbols grow naturally in you, without forcing, without jumping to conclusions.

DREAM WORK ILLUSTRATION: THE MONASTERY

As an example of making associations we have the following dream and some of the actual associations that the dreamer made in her notebook when she was working on it. Because we have limited time and space, I will transcribe only a few of the images from her dream with some of their associations.

The woman who had this dream comes from an Italian Catholic family. As she grew into adulthood she found herself rebelling against her Latin background and her childhood religion. She became involved in Zen Buddhist philosophy and meditation. This dream signaled a return to her cultural and religious roots, yet a graduation out of her childhood version of them. It showed her that she could make a synthesis of East and West within her own self that was true to her own character.

Dream

I am in a monastic cloister, in a room or cell attached to the chapel. I am separated from the people and the rest of the chapel by a grille. Mass begins. I participate alone in my cell. I sit with crossed legs, *zazen* style, but holding my rosary. I hear the murmurs of the responses through the grille. The voices are tranquil. I close my eyes and I too receive communion, although no one and nothing physical enters my cell. The mass finishes. I become aware of flowers blooming at the side of my chamber. I feel a deep serenity.

Step One: My Associations

Monastery	Religious life; formal religious life; community, my childhood religion; contemplation; sacrifice, medieval cloisters in Italy and Spain; separation from the world; Zen monastery I almost joined.
Room/cell	Container; womb; the basic component of life-forms; protection; separation from the collective; individuation; the path that must be traveled alone, outside of any collective identity or comfort.
Mass	*En masse* = collective form of religious experience; group worship through intermediary priest; religious form of my particular collective; form I left to individuate. One step removed = need to participate in religious experience yet not be identified with collective, outer form of the inner experience.

Communion	Last Supper, Christ's sacrifice, sacrament, that communion song I've always hated; fainting during three-hour fast; mystical union; to become one with = com-union; transubstantiation = transformation; comes in *nonphysical* form = must be experienced on the inner plane, inwardly rather than collectively.
Zazen	Practicing stillness; the familiarity I felt with the practice from the very first, like going home; practice without dogma; experience rather than doctrine; foreign to my upbringing; grief when I saw I couldn't "belong" to Zen collective, either; Zen monastery I had to say no to.
Grille	Separation; partial separation; interaction with the collective world but differentiated interaction; separate identity; separate consciousness.

This gives you a sample of the wealth of material that will flow spontaneously from the unconscious when we really focus on the dream image and look for every association that comes to mind. We have all this material, even though we have not yet gone through all the images.

If you have looked carefully at this woman's associations so far, you may already see the basic relationships that are forming among the images and the various associations that seem to make coherent sense together. You will see how these associations led eventually to her interpretation.

This dream advised the dreamer of the right and the necessity for her to be an individual. The emphasis in the dream was on her living out her religious nature; she had to participate in the mystery, yet not by identifying with a particular external, collective version of religion. In the dream she participated, but remained separate from the group and the group version of religious experience. This was not because she was an elitist, but because that is her nature and her way.

The detail of receiving communion without any physical contact was consistent with her understanding of her dream. She had to experience the immediacy of the Godhead, the transformation, but she had to experience it inwardly and in her individual way, not by identifying with a collective, cultural version of the experience. In her associations she remembered that she had also considered joining a Buddhist monastery in order to be able to join in the community, belong to something, and follow in a collectively defined way. But she could not do it with Buddhism any more than she could with Catholicism.

The good news in all of this for her was that she could return to her Catholic and Christian heritage but with a new understanding of it that allowed her to participate and to see the essential spirit at the center of the cultural and collective forms. She could be in community, yet not be swallowed by it. She could participate, yet remain an individual going her own unique way.

The flowers that bloom in her cell at the end of the mass she found to be a symbol of new life and new consciousness resulting from the synthesis that she has made in the dream between her childhood religion and her adult experience of the spirit. More accurately speaking, the flowers express the synthesis itself. Such a symbol points to that archetype—the self—that transcends the opposites by revealing the central reality behind them and thereby unites them.

Flowers are not only symbols of the feminine but also of the unified self: in Christianity, the rose that represents Christ; in Eastern religions, the thousand-petaled lotus that portrays the One. By this dreamer's way, which is the path of stillness, she brought the flower of the self into bloom in her life. She found the universal kernel of spirit that is at the center of both her Christian roots and her Zen experience—that transcends both and is not identified with the *outer form* of either.

Some important things happened to this woman as an aftermath to this dream. When we get to the fourth step in dream work, which is to do a ritual to express the meaning of your dream, we will return to this Dream of the Monastery. This dreamer's ritual for her dream, and the events that followed, are very instructive.

USING ARCHETYPAL AMPLIFICATION

There is another way of finding associations to dream images: *archetypal amplification*. It is basically a process of gathering information about the archetypes that appear in our dreams by going to sources such as myths, fairy tales, and ancient religious traditions.

I have already given you a simple example in the Dream of the Monastery. I spontaneously associated the flowers that appeared in this woman's room with their role in Christianity, Buddhism, and other religions as symbols of the archetypal self. That, in turn, keyed us into the other information that we already know about the self—that it is the transcendent function that combines the opposites, that draws the fragments of our totality into a unity. And all of this, of course, added greatly to our sense of the meaning and power of the dream.

Jung became aware of the archetypes by observing that the same primordial symbols appear equally in ancient myths and religions and in the dreams of modern people. He was startled to find that images appear in people's dreams that refer to some very ancient symbol, perhaps from a completely different culture, that could not have been known to the conscious mind of the dreamer. From these experiences he began to see that our dreams draw on universal, primordial sources that are deep in the collective unconscious of all humankind. We can often see more clearly how the symbols in our dreams are tied to those universal streams of energy when we encounter the symbols, as Jung did, in myth, religion, and other ancient sources.

It becomes possible to go to a myth where the archetype appears and find the collective associations that the human race as a whole has to that archetype. We can read in the myth all the qualities in us that are contained in the archetype and that are associated with its symbols.

Jung has demonstrated that myths and fairy tales are symbolic manifestations of the unconscious, just as dreams are. In a sense they are the collective dreams of the human race: They reflect the collective unconscious of a tribe, a people, or a culture rather than the local, personal unconscious of one individual. Therefore they are rich sources of information on the archetypes. They go back to the preconscious era, when the human race was closer to its archetypal roots. We may also look to esoteric philosophical traditions, such as medieval alchemy and ancient astrology, as sources of information regarding the archetypes.

The archetype that appears in your dream is a universal quality, a stream of energy that finds its way into every human being. As the archetype is universal, so is its imagery. Each archetype tends to express itself with its own characteristic symbolism.

The image of the Wise Old Man, for example, is ubiquitous throughout all cultures and races. His image varies from myth to myth, culture to culture. But once you learn to recognize him, you see him in the dreams of a Hindu as well as those of a Westerner.

He may take the form of Saint Peter holding the key to heaven, as he did in one of Jung's dreams. He may appear as a personification of God the Father, as in the vision of Michelangelo on the ceiling of the Sistine Chapel; in the dream of a Buddhist as a *roshi* (master) or *bodhisattva* (demigod); in a Hindu's dream as a *guru* or a *sunyasin* (ascetic holy man).

There is a common quality that runs through the symbols of the Wise Man—a feeling of wisdom that transcends generations, agelessness in the sense of being outside the flow of time. Here we find him as he appears in a modern myth from the hand of J. R. R. Tolkien:

His hair was dark as the shadows of twilight and upon it was set a circlet of silver; his eyes were grey as a clear evening, and in them was a light like the light of stars. Venerable he seemed as a king crowned with many winters, and yet hale as a tried warrior in the fullness of his strength. . . (Tolkien, *Fellowship of the Ring*, p. 299)

Archetypal amplification begins with recognizing that an archetypal presence has entered into one's dream. The dream that contains an archetype often has a mythical quality. Instead of scenes that seem like the everyday world, the dream takes you to a place that feels ancient, from another time, or like a fairy tale. You find yourself in a legendary place like Baghdad in the time of genies, magic carpets, and magicians. Another sign is that things are bigger than life or smaller than life. Archetypes may also present themselves as otherworldly animals: talking lions, griffins, dragons, flying horses.

Archetypal figures often have an aura of royalty or divinity. The ancient Greeks personified the archetypes as gods who created the world by shaping the contours of fate or as the heroes and heroines who were caught up in the forces that the gods set in motion.

The Great Mother quality in human nature appears as Aphrodite, goddess of sensual love; Hera, goddess of home and hearth; Demeter, goddess of agriculture. Turning to the Hindu world, we find the Great Mother personified as Kali, the terrible goddess who both blesses and destroys, gives life and takes it back, in the eternal cycle of nature.

These manifestations of the great archetypes show up in the dreams of ordinary mortals. Each of us is a channel through which these archetypal forces must find their way into concrete existence. We *incarnate* the archetypes with our physical lives. Our individual lives are the containers in which they materialize on the face of the earth, the battlegrounds where they fight their eternal, cosmic battles, the stages on which they perform the universal drama that becomes, in one particularized form, every human life.

Once we recognize that a figure is an archetype, the next step is to go to the myths and other sources where the same archetype appears. The figure or events in your dream may spark a memory of a passage in the Bible or a great tale from the days of King Arthur. You go to that source and see what it tells you about this great archetype that has come to you in your dream. What are its characteristics? What is its role in human life? If it is the Great Mother, for example, you go to the myths of the Greek goddesses who personify her, to the manifestations of Kali, to the varied epiphanies of the Holy Virgin.

As you amplify the information on your dream figure, you continue what you have already done with your personal associations: Write down the associations that come to you from the mythical sources. If they elicit energy from inside you, if they make sense, try them out. See what they have to say about who you are and what forces are at work in you.

USING PERSONAL ASSOCIATIONS

This is a good point at which to caution you against using so-called dream-books and dictionaries of symbolism as substitutes for your own personal associations.

Many people unthinkingly turn to a dictionary of symbols each time they try to understand a dream. They look up each symbol from the dream, write down the standard meanings the dictionary serves up, and then believe that they have "interpreted" their dream. If you use this kind of approach you will never get to the individual, special meaning that your dream has for you.

These approaches are based on an erroneous assumption: that every symbol has one, standard, collective meaning that is true for every dream and every person. If that were so, it would be very convenient indeed; but it isn't.

It is plain foolishness to believe in ready-made, systematic guides to dream interpretation, as if one could simply buy a reference book and look up a particular symbol. *No dream symbol can be separated from the individual who dreams it.* . . . Each individual varies so much in the way that his unconscious complements or compensates his conscious mind that it is impossible to be sure how far dreams and their symbols can be classified at all. . . .

It is true that there are dreams and single symbols (I should prefer to call them "motifs") that are typical and often occur. Among such motifs are falling, flying, . . . running hard yet getting nowhere. . . . But I must stress again that these are motifs that must be considered in the context of the dream itself, not as self-explanatory ciphers.
(Jung, *Man and His Symbols*, p. 53) [Emphasis added.]

Every symbol in your dream has a special, individual connotation that belongs to you alone, just as the dream is ultimately yours alone. Even when a symbol has a collective or universal meaning, it still has a personal coloration for you and can be fully explained only from within you.

This is why it is so important that you do this first step thoroughly. Find the associations that are yours, that come from your own unconscious. Don't accept standardized interpretations as a substitute.

This advice is even more important when we get into archetypal amplification. People can get so overinvolved with searching for mythic connections that they forget that they also have personal associations to the symbols. This is the point at which the temptation is so strong to turn to a dictionary of symbolism, find out what the myths say about the symbol, and stop there.

If I don't find my *personal* connection to the archetype, then all this is pointless. The archetype is present in me, acting through me, living its life through mine. When it appears in my dream, it means that something is going on between my ego and that archetype; something is trying to evolve. I have to pin it down, see how it relates to *my* life, now, today.

It isn't enough to say, "Ah! That is a symbol of the Great Mother." It isn't enough to hang an abstract label on the dream person—Great Mother, anima, shadow—and then walk away from it. We have to push further. We have to ask: "What is this archetype doing today in my personal life? What does this have to do with me, individually?"

Strictly speaking, it should not be necessary for anyone to get involved in researching myths, comparative religion, alchemy, and so forth in order to find the universal level of meaning for a symbol. When the unconscious uses a symbol, it inherently contains within itself the meaning of the symbol. It already knows its own reference to the symbol. Therefore, if you pursue your personal associations to the dream image, the unconscious will, sooner or later, produce the archetypal connections that apply.

Nevertheless, it is a great aid to know what the symbol has meant to others, and how it has appeared in collective myths and folktales. This knowledge can shorten the process. It can also act as confirmation of the personal associations that spring spontaneously out of you.

Step Two: Dynamics

In the second step we connect each dream image to a specific dynamic in our inner lives. We identify the parts of our inner self that appear as the images in the dream.

The reason for making this connection is a fundamental one: We need to figure out what is going on inside ourselves that is represented by the situation in the dream. If we could not tie the dream to specific events, feelings, or other dynamics in our lives, the dream would be pointless. It would be mere entertainment.

To perform this step, we go back to the beginning and deal with each image, one at a time. For each image ask: "What part of me is that? Where have I seen it functioning in my life lately? Where do I see that same trait in my personality? Who is it, inside me, who feels like that or behaves like that?" Then, write down each example you can think of in which that inner part of you has been expressing itself in your life.

By *inner dynamics* we mean anything that goes on inside you, any energy system that lives and acts from within you. It may be an emotional event, such as a surge of anger. It may be an inner conflict, an inner personality acting through you, a feeling, an attitude, a mood.

Suppose we are working with this dream in which the word *blue* came up. You write all your associations with that word, and the one that "clicks" for you is *depression*—bad mood, having "the blues." Now, during the second step, you look for the "blue" quality inside you: "Where is that blue quality in me? Where am I blue? Where have I been depressed?" The answer may come to you: "I've been depressed at my job." Questioning yourself in this way, you begin to see how this image relates to an actual part of you.

Often we are unaware that depression has seized us. We are so busy that we don't have time to focus on what is going on inside. In another case, something very good could be developing inwardly—a new strength emerging, a wound being healed, a chronic fear evaporating—that we fail to appreciate. We have to ask ourselves: "What goes on *inside me* that this dream speaks of?" Then we wake up to the paths that our inner lives are taking.

We must find that specific inner event at the deepest level of our lives. And we need to find *specific examples*. We are not finished with this step until we find actual examples from our lives that correspond to the events in the dream.

We also need to keep writing. There was an old tradition in the Christian Church that one had not prayed unless one's lips had moved. This idea expresses a psychological truth: Something *physical* has to happen. This is why it is so important that you write your examples down on paper. When you physically write those examples, the connections with your dream become clear and definite.

TAKING DREAMS INWARDLY

At this stage in dream work there is always a question whether the dream is commenting on one's *inner* life or on the external situation. We sometimes express it by asking if the dream is to be taken "inwardly."

Most dreams are representations of what goes on inside the dreamer. Dreams usually speak of the evolution of forces inside us, the conflicts of values and viewpoints there, the different unconscious energy systems that are trying to be heard, trying to find their way into our conscious lives.

The overall subject of our dreams is, ultimately, the inner process of individuation. Most dreams, in one way or another, are portrayals of our individual journeys toward wholeness. They show us the stages along the way—the adventures, obstacles, conflicts, and reconciliations that lead finally to a sense of the self. Every dream, in some way, either shows our effort to integrate some unconscious part of ourselves into consciousness or our resistance against the inner self, the ways we set up conflict with it rather than learn from it. This is the primary subject that our dreams are reporting on, and this is what we should look for in our dreams.

At first, many people find it difficult to think of a complete inner world, existing within us and paralleling the outer world; for some, it is hard to see that our dream lives are mostly concerned with the inner world. Our culture teaches us to focus on the external world, so we jump to the conclusion that our dreams are talking about something on the outside. This is a collective prejudice we suffer from: We spontaneously assume that only the *outer* world has any importance.

The true significance of the inner world becomes more clear when we begin to realize that almost everything we do, every reaction we have, every decision we make, every relationship we form, ultimately results from our inner qualities and inner dynamics. Everything is controlled by the huge energy systems that propel us from within, that determine most of what we think and do.

If you take your dreams as a reflection of the unconscious dynamics within you, you are most likely to get to the heart of the matter; if, however, you apply the dream on the external level, it usually turns out to be superficial. It is on the inner level that you can change life-patterns most profoundly; it is at the inner level that your dream is usually aimed.

There *are* a few dreams—they appear once in a great while—that are directed at something *outside* the dreamer and don't have anything to do directly with the dreamer's inner life. Sometimes people dream of great battles or disasters just before a war breaks out. Sometimes a person dreams of something happening to a friend or relative who is a great distance away, and later discovers that the event actually took place in the other person's life. As a general rule, however, symbols in a dream turn out to apply to the dreamer's own interior life. So, that is the best assumption to work from.

I remember a patient who came to me with a dream in which his friend drove at a crazy speed and crashed into a building. He feared that the dream foretold a car accident; he wondered if he should warn his friend. I told him that it was most likely that the dream used the image of his friend to symbolize an inflation in his own life—a runaway compulsion or "power trip" or enthusiasm that was about to get out of control. In the meantime, as a precaution, I advised him not to go riding with his fast-driving friend.

As it turned out, our interpretation was correct. The dreamer got a new job, started feeling like a big man, lost his head, and got into something of a "power trip." Fortunately, since the dream had warned him of it, he spotted the ego inflation and brought it under control before it became too obnoxious. As for the friend who was shown crashing his car in the dream—he is still driving around like a madman.

The best solution I have come up with, after years of wrestling with this issue, is this: Always begin by applying your dream inwardly. Start by assuming that your dream represents an inner dynamic, and work with it on that basis. Later, if it turns out that the dream does refer to an external situation, adjust your interpretation accordingly.

There are good reasons for taking this approach, the first being, as we have said, the simple fact that most dreams refer to something going on inside the dreamer. It makes more sense to start off with that assumption, therefore; otherwise, you are liable to miss the main import of your dream.

Second, we have to compensate for our collective prejudice in favor of the external world. The only way we can do this is to force ourselves, in a disciplined way, to look for the inner meaning of the dream. As soon as we start to apply the dream to our external lives, we get lost in speculations about people we know and all the situations we are involved with; we never get back to exploring the real subject: the situation *inside* that is creating the situation outside.

Even when our dreams make some direct comment on an external situation, you may assume that there is an inner dynamic involved. In some way, your relationship to that external person or situation is being affected by some fantasy that has seized you, some inner attitude that dominates you, some belief or ideal in your inner mind.

It is fruitless to waste your time trying to understand an external situation unless you also identify the psychological patterns within you that affect it. And it is toward those patterns that your dreams usually point.

Still, people often get confused over this issue, because the unconscious has the habit of *borrowing* images from the external situation and using those images to symbolize something that is going on inside the dreamer. Your dream may borrow the image of your next-door neighbor, your spouse, or your parent and use that image to refer to something inside you.

For illustration, let us suppose that a man is extremely prejudiced and opinionated. One night he dreams and the image of his wife appears in the dream trying to argue him out of some of his attitudes. It happens that his wife is an open-minded person with a flexible, inquisitive intelligence who is interested in other people's viewpoints. In this case the dream is probably using his wife's image to tell him that he needs to be less opinionated, less defensive, and more open to new ideas. The capacity for this is identified with his inner feminine side, so his unconscious chooses his wife's image to represent it in the dream. By using his wife as a symbol, the dream tries to wake him up to possibility within himself.

The natural reaction is to think: "Since my wife is in this dream, it is obviously talking about my wife or about my relationship to my wife." It is a natural conclusion, but, in practice, it usually isn't so. The dream is most likely to use the image of the wife to represent a quality in the dreamer, a conflict in the dreamer, or something evolving in him that has little to do, directly, with his external wife.

In this situation the dreamer has several things to understand: First, he needs to see that he has an *inner* wife, who is distinct from his outer wife and lives in the inner world and is a part of him. Then, he needs to stop blaming his physical wife for his conflicts with his inner wife—which turn out to be conflicts within himself. Finally, he needs to take his inner wife, his inner feminine, seriously. He needs to try to understand what part of himself she represents and what it is that she is trying to communicate to him.

This is probably the single most important principle in dream work—the one that determines whether you will find the wisdom in your dreams. We have to recognize that dreams are intricate tapestries of symbolism, and each image represents something going on within our own selves.

Sometimes the urge to take the image literally is overwhelming, especially if you are in conflict with the person who has appeared in your dream. We want to use the dream as an excuse to blame the external person or to congratulate ourselves on how right we are. But if we resist that temptation, and instead look for the quality inside ourselves that the dream speaks of in symbols, we learn amazing things about ourselves that we could never otherwise have seen.

CONNECTING IMAGES TO SPECIFIC CHARACTERISTICS

Probably the most immediate and practical way to connect a particular image to yourself is to ask what traits you have in common with the image: What are the main characteristics of the person in the dream? How would you describe his or her character and personality? Where do you find those same traits in you?

If the image is of an angry person, where do you find an angry quality in you? If it is happy-go-lucky, where do you find that same quality in yourself?

We all have a set of fundamental characteristics from which everything else in our personalities derive: These basics include our feelings, belief systems, attitudes, and patterns of behavior and the values we adhere to. All these traits show up in our dreams and can be identified if we look for them.

Every dream is a portrait of the dreamer. You may think of your dream as a mirror that reflects your inner character—the aspects of your personality of which you are not fully aware. Once we understand this, we can also see that every trait portrayed in our dreams has to exist in us, somewhere, regardless of whether we are aware of it or admit it. Whatever characteristics the dream figures have, whatever behavior they engage in, is also true of the dreamer in some way.

By this, I don't mean that the trait or behavior shown in the dream is *literally* true of the dreamer exactly as it is portrayed in the dream. Dreams often speak in extremes: They try to compensate for our lack of awareness of a quality by picturing it in extreme, dramatic imagery.

For example, if there is a thief in your dream, it doesn't literally mean that you are a thief. The dream uses this dramatic image to get your attention and tell you that you need to wake up to something inside you. It may be that you have been dishonest with yourself in some way. If so, you need to be aware of it and deal with it. But the image of the thief may also mean that you have repressed some fine quality in yourself, figuratively "locked it out" of your life, and the only way it can get back into your life is to "break in" like a burglar.

Because we often repress the best parts of ourselves and think of them as "negative" qualities, some of the richest parts of the self—even the voice of God itself—can only partake in our lives by "stealing" our time, stealing our energy through compulsions and neurosis, and slipping into our lives in the unprotected places where our guard is down:

> Of the times and seasons, brethren, you have no need that I write you. For yourselves know perfectly that the Day of the Lord cometh as a *thief in the night*. (Paul, to the Thessalonians)

Our egos divide the world into positive and negative, good and bad. Most aspects of our shadows, these qualities that we see as "negative," would in fact be valuable strengths if we made them conscious. Characteristics that look immoral, barbaric, or embarrassing to us are the "negative" side of a valuable energy, a capacity we could make use of. You will never find anything in the unconscious that will not be useful and good when it is made conscious and brought to the right level.

What part of you will be hidden behind this symbol, the thief? Perhaps a lively trickster, with all sorts of surprising talents. Perhaps a juvenile delinquent in you who has never been allowed to grow up and put his heroic urge into something useful and mature. Perhaps it is Dionysus, who has had to hide out in the unconscious because you have no natural place for his ecstatic and lyrical spirit in the midst of your purposive life.

Only you will be able to say what part of you is represented by this symbol if it appears in your dream—for it is your own unconscious that holds the clues. But you may be sure that if you give it its place, and hear what it has to say, it will be revealed as a valuable part of your inner self.

Curiously, people usually resist their good qualities even more emphatically than they resist facing their negative qualities. There may be a character in your dream who behaves in a noble and courageous way. Since that inner person is part of you, its qualities are also yours. So long as you are facing your negative and immature traits squarely, you also have a duty to acknowledge the fine qualities in yourself, and to live them consciously.

LOOKING AT BELIEFS, ATTITUDES, AND VALUES

Our dreams constantly speak to us of our beliefs and attitudes. They are of such crucial importance because they largely determine what we do, how we relate to people, and how we react to most situations. Most of us are not remotely aware of how much we are controlled by our beliefs, even less aware of how unconscious our attitude systems are.

No one decides what beliefs and attitudes he or she will start off with. We all begin our lives with a set of attitudes that are dictated to us by the world outside us—family, tribe, or society. Generally, we don't know we have them. If we are consciously aware of them as our beliefs, we assume that they are right; it rarely occurs to us to question them.

At a certain point our dreams begin to challenge them and point them out to us, for the process of inner growth demands that we examine consciously everything that motivates us. If you look at the belief systems floating around in your dreams, you may find a power-mad dictator, a great general, a saint, or a sage living in you, with a complete matching set of attitudes. When this image appears, you should ask: "What set of beliefs, what opinions, does this character function out of? Do I unconsciously hold that same opinion without realizing it?"

Napoleon would represent a particular set of beliefs, a point of view about the nature of reality. The image of Gandhi symbolizes a completely different attitude about life, people, and power. You may find both coexisting inside you.

A liberal young man who believed that he had no interest in worldly power but only in service to the poor had the following dream on the day he received his professional license.

Dream

When I walk to the place to keep my appointment, it turns out to be a used-car lot. I stand on the sidewalk. Suddenly Richard Nixon walks up. He seems to be a salesman. He slaps me on the back and says: "Alright! Let's see some enthusiasm! If you're going to be a real professional, you've got to start learning the basic tricks for manipulating people. Learn to think positive. Put on a suit, look the part, feel the part. Get out there and sell yourself. That's the way to success."

To the dreamer, this dream was extremely sarcastic, as dreams often can be. In his conscious attitudes he disliked politicians, people who grasped after worldly power or used "motivational techniques," euphemisms for manipulating people through the hard sell. But here, in his dream, he found that he not only had a hidden power drive, he also had a whole belief system living in secret within. In spite of himself, he secretly believed, or part of him believed, in "getting ahead," going after rather cheap versions of earthly power and using Madison Avenue hype and manipulative charm to get there.

There was no mystery about what this dream was saying. The dream figure obligingly detailed the attitudes he stood for, much to the dreamer's chagrin. Such a dream is embarrassing but also infinitely valuable to the dreamer. It is worth pure gold to know what you are *really* up to, underneath your professed ideals. The dream enables you to make a conscious, ethical choice—either accept the attitudes in your dreams, or renounce them; or, best of all, make an intelligent synthesis.

In practice, neither the conscious attitude of your ego nor the unconscious attitude of your inner self is the final answer. The attitude that is true to your character lies somewhere in between. In fact, if your unconscious attitude seems exaggerated, it usually means that the unconscious is compensating for an equally off-balance, exaggerated position in the ego.

This is one way you can tell when your ego has taken an extreme, off-center position that is not true to your actual character: You will find an exaggerated position in the unconscious, compensating your ego's position. The unconscious attitude is always off-center exactly to the same extent that the ego attitude is. As the ego attitude becomes more moderate, the unconscious attitude also relaxes toward the center.

In the case of this last dream, the dreamer was lost in glorious idealism. He took no thought for anything practical or for how he would make a living. The unconscious reacted by producing a compensatory attitude of pure, ravenous materialism. When he scaled his idealism down to something more practical, he found his secret power drive took on a less exaggerated form.

Dreams also talk about our values: our feelings about what is good, desirable, beautiful, true, moral, or honorable. Ultimately our values are the qualities that we seek most in life, the standards that give our lives a sense of meaning. Our values express what is highest and most important to us.

We all have many value systems coexisting inside us, and all are in conflict with each other to some degree. My ego may feel that work alone is virtuous and that wasting time is immoral. But another part of me has a different set of values. It wants to go to parties and would be happiest on a tropical island. My ego may value thrift and practicality above all, but another part of me feels that I will just die unless I can buy an expensive new suit or a luxurious car.

I learned something about this in a powerful way from a short, insignificant-looking dream that I had years ago when I first began work as a psychologist.

Dream

I am stealing a newspaper from a vending machine. I suddenly wake up to what I am doing, and I feel guilty.

This was a situation in which my ego held to a certain set of values but I then discovered that quite another value system ruled somewhere else in me. On the conscious level, I don't believe in stealing—not even a newspaper, which in those times would have cost only five cents. Yet the dream was hurling in my face this accusation: "You are a crook! Part of you wants to steal!"

What could I do with this? I felt devastated and guilty about this dream. I tried to find where in my life I was unconsciously stealing. Finally it occurred to me to look more closely at the other details in the dream. What about the newspaper?

I mulled it over. What does the newspaper represent? To me, it represents collective platitudes, collective opinions, gossip, scandals raked up to serve as news, propaganda. I saw that I was stealing something of very low quality, at least in the view of my unconscious. The dream objected to *what* I was stealing as much as to the act itself.

Finally I made the connections: At that time I was just starting in my profession. I was very unsure of myself. I was looking in awe at authority figures and trying to fit into every group, every clique, that might give me some feeling of belonging or of being "someone." I listened to all the collective opinions, the collective platitudes, and the gossip around these people, and I repeated it. Sometimes I repeated it as though it were *my* information, *my* conclusions, *my* viewpoint.

I was "stealing" all this collective nonsense because I wasn't thinking for myself: I was taking it from others, free of charge, and serving it up as though it were my own. I was not paying the price for having my own ideas and wouldn't dare think for myself because I so desperately wanted to belong. It was in this sense that I was "stealing" a lot of junk that wasn't worth having in the first place.

This is not an unusual kind of stealing: Most people do it at one time or another when they want to fit into a group. But my unconscious protested, and used this dream to throw cold water in my face. Psychologically, it woke me up.

This dream is a good example for showing that we need to do each step of dream work thoroughly. We need to work with every image and overlook no details. We don't know which detail may provide the key that opens up the deepest meaning of the dream. I spent a full week wrestling with this dream before I had enough sense to ask myself what the symbol *newspaper* meant to me.

Behavior patterns are among the most important personal traits that show up in our dreams. Our behavior, like our values, comes from within. Most of the time we are not very aware of what we do, or why we do it. Our behavior is generated by the values that we serve, by those inner beliefs and attitudes that we have discussed. One of the best ways to discover what you really believe in, what value you are really serving, is to watch your own behavior.

For example, you may *think* that you believe in saving money. Most people say they do, if asked. But, in actual practice, if you spend your entire paycheck and never save a cent, that reveals a completely different set of beliefs controlling you, a different value system than the one you profess.

Dreams are wonderful reporters of our unconscious patterns of behavior. If I tend to be opinionated and combative, my dreams will eventually show me a dream figure who is combative. My dreams will give me an idea of how I must sound to other people. If I constantly say yes to everyone when I ought to say no, my dreams may show me someone who does that. And the messes that he gets into will bear an uncanny resemblance to the messes I regularly find myself in.

So, when you see a pattern of behavior in a dream, look for it diligently in your personal daily life. Somewhere you will find it, and behind your behavior, you will find an attitude.

LOCATING INNER PERSONALITIES

A good way to connect to the inner parts of yourself is to think of each dream figure as an actual person living inside you. Think of each person in your dream as one of the autonomous personalities that coexist within your psyche and combine to make up your total self.

Then the question becomes: "Where have I seen this *person* at work in my life lately? Where in my life have I seen her (if she's a woman) doing what she did in the dream? What part of me is it that feels like that, thinks like that, behaves like that?"

If she brings conflict in the dream, then try to find the part of your personality that is in conflict or rebellion. If she seeks relatedness and affection in the dream, look for the part of you that has been looking for friendship, loving, falling in love. If she pulls you out of the gutter, as did the Girl with the Sparkling Eyes in the dream that follows Step Three, then look in your life to see where some strength, some interest, some insight has pulled you out of the gutter recently. And there you find her at work in your life.

You may see, as you look at your dream person, that he or she is a manifestation of one of the basic personality structures, one of the primary energy systems, that make up the psyche. A woman in your dream may exactly fit the description of the shadow, if you are a woman, or fit the description of anima, if you are a man. This discovery will give you some added hints about where you can expect to find this inner person in action in your life.

But if a man, for example, finds that a dream-person is his anima, his work does not stop there. He has to find specifically where she is active in his life. He has to find the feelings he has felt, the flow of fantasy that has seized him, the mood he has been in, the encounter with the inner world—whatever it is that shows exactly what has been going on in his life that he associates with the soul-feminine.

It is a mistake to jump to conclusions and to call your inner person *anima* or *shadow* or one of these terms if you are not really sure. For every dream-person who fits clearly within one of the archetypes, there are many others who don't: They are just persons in your dream. In that case, don't force them into a mold. Let them be who they are.

In order to find this dream-person inside yourself, a good place to begin is to make a description. Write out what kind of person you think this is, what the person's main characteristics and personality are, what the person wants and means to you. Then you can look for the part of your personality that matches the description.

If the person is intolerant and moralistic, you look for the part of your character that is intolerant or puritanical. There you will find your dream-person, living in you and through you.

Often your dream gives the person a name. If not, you can invent a name that seems to capture the person's character. Or you can use a descriptive name. If it is a masculine figure, it may be Brave Warrior, Wise Elder, Old Miser, Sneaky Crook, Juvenile Delinquent, Young Prince, Trickster, Tribal Brother. If this is a feminine figure you may find yourself calling her Wise Mother, Tyrant Mother, Earth Mother, Faithful Sister, My Lady Soul, Lady of the Sparkling Eyes. If she fits the mythical role, you may give her a mythical name: Helen, Iseult of the White Hands, Guinevere.

It is best if we get acquainted with our inner personalities *as persons in their own right* before we start putting distance between us and them by using psychological classifications and jargon. You will get much closer to your inner feminine if you know her as "Lady Ingrid," for example, and think of her as a special and interesting being who lives inside you, than if you call her "the anima" and turn her into a clinical abstraction.

Thus, if a feminine figure appears in a man's dream he should not start describing her from the standard texts on anima. He must allow her to describe herself and be the unique, individual being who came to visit him in his dream. He must allow her to have her individuality.

In the same way, when a woman finds a masculine figure in her dream, she should not jump to the conclusion that this is her animus, and start automatically applying all the doctrines that pertain to the animus. She should get close to this inner person, find out what his character and functions are, learn from him directly what information or qualities he has to offer and what his role is in her inner world.

IDENTIFYING OTHER INNER REALITIES

Of course, the images in dreams are not only the dream-people. There are also places, buildings, animals, colors, numbers, objects, and abstract geometric symbols. Dreams present an infinite variety of images, and all of them are used to symbolize, in some way, the flow of your inner life.

In one way or another, you can always picture the dream image as something located inside yourself. For example, if it is a place, then it is a place inside you, and you can locate it. A place in a dream may represent a "place to stand" in a moral sense—an ethical position you need to take. A place like the Castle of the Holy Grail represents a level of spiritual consciousness and also a goal toward which your inner growth is moving you. A dream place may also represent an emotional environment, a set of circumstances, or a sphere of influence.

Remember our preoccupation with the blue room? The main association was an emotional environment. The ego was sitting in the midst of a blue feeling, a depression.

One of the most frequent uses of places in dreams is to show you whose "turf" you are on, whose influence you are under. So a good way to understand the significance of a place is to ask who it belongs to.

Ancient astrologers formed the practice of speaking symbolically of the "house" of Mars or the "house" of Saturn or some other planet. It meant that your psyche had fallen under that planetary influence: You were visiting in its house. When you enter into one of these symbolic houses, you enter a different psychological environment, a different field of energy.

In the same way, if you find yourself in the house of your maternal grandmother, you know that you are in the sphere of influence of the Great Mother. It means that, for better or for worse, you were under her spell on the evening when your dream was hatching in the unconscious. It may mean that you are on the verge of a great revelation of the Queen of Heaven. If you are lying in the gutter in front of her house, however, it more likely means that you are caught in the negative side of your mother complex—caught in passivity and dependency. Only the circumstances of your dream will tell you for sure what it means to be in the "house of the Mother."

If the house belongs to you, it probably represents your *ego-house*—the field of consciousness of the ego, the world the ego builds up around itself, made up of what you know, what you think, what you believe, and the walls erected to protect you from the unconscious. If your house is invaded from the outside, it generally means that the ego's world is being invaded by forces from the unconscious. You are being confronted, perhaps, with realities, values, and parts of your own self that you have managed to avoid until now.

If you find yourself in a country ruled by an evil sorcerer or a military dictator, it may mean that you are under the control of your power drive. If you ride through a blessed land ruled by an ancient and wise king or queen, the dream is giving you a foretaste of what life feels like when we live attuned to the archetypal self, aligned with the highest wisdom within ourselves.

What about animals? If it is an animal, you may think of it as an animal instinct or animal consciousness that lives somewhere inside you, buried in the deepest primordial, prehuman roots of the psyche. It is one of the energy systems from which you are constructed and has to be taken into account. It barks from time to time if it is neglected.

Just as people have characteristics that you can identify with, so do animals. Animals, like many other archetypal symbols, have both positive and negative connotations. Dogs are a good example. Dogs are pack animals, like wolves and coyotes. A dog in your dream could refer to the human tendency to "follow the pack," to get so involved with groups and collectivity and "belonging" that we cease to develop as individuals or to have an inner life. For humans, we find, are also pack animals. It is a strong instinct in us, one that brings out both the best and the worst in human nature.

On the other hand, dogs are supremely loyal. The humble image of a dog in your dream may refer to a noble quality in you, a capacity for the deepest loyalty. Sometimes it is difficult to tell from a dream whether the positive or the negative connotation is to be taken. Sometimes the dog may be a warning, sometimes a powerful affirmation. Usually some very small detail in the dream will tell us which way to take the symbol.

Jung found that animals often represent primitive physical and instinctual energy systems within us. They may correspond to a physical need for food, rest, or exercise or a need for erotic or sensual experience. A fight with a threatening animal in a dream may signal a conflict between the needs of your deep, instinctual side and the "civilized" attitudes of your conscious mind.

When they appear in mythical form, animals may also represent the great archetypes or the highest stages of spiritual consciousness and development. The elephant represents, in Hindu symbolism, the highest manifestation of the true self, and the elephant sometimes appears in the dream of a Westerner with the same meaning. In my own dreams, the white cobra comes to me often as a manifestation of the self, of the highest consciousness within me.

The examples I have given you in the last few pages represent only a tiny sampling of the infinite opportunities you have for connecting your dream images accurately to your inner self and the dynamics of your inner life. There could never be enough space—in this book or any other book—to cover all the symbols that might arise and the various ways they might connect to your life. And if we tried to do that, we would only mislead. For, as I have been emphasizing so strongly, the real connections between your dream symbols and your inner life can only truly come out of you, out of the fertile soil of your own unconscious.

DREAM WORK ILLUSTRATION: THE GIRL WITH THE SPARKLING EYES

As an example of how we can do this step with an actual dream, I will now present another dream, together with the connections that could be made to the inner life of the dreamer.

This dream was brought to me by a college student, twenty-two years old at the time. He came for analysis when he was unable to continue college because of a severe neurosis. He had reached the point where he couldn't study or pass his exams, and he was in a state of despair.

This was the first dream in the analysis. It beautifully depicted the state he was in, showed us what inner systems were involved, and pointed him in the direction he needed to go. The dream predicted the dramatic healing of the neurosis, which took place almost immediately after he began doing inner work. He is one of those people who can't live without an inner life, but once he recognized this, everything changed rapidly. He finished his education and now leads an unusually full and useful life.

In honor of the manifestation of his anima who appears here, I call the dream the Dream of the Girl with the Sparkling Eyes.

The Dream of the Girl with the Sparkling Eyes

I was lying in the street in front of my grandmother's house. An auto came from behind containing my sister and her friend. I was afraid that the car would run over me, and I rolled toward the curb as quickly as I could. Then they were beside me. My sister asked me if I would like her to arrange a date for me with one of her other friends. She mentioned a couple of names. I couldn't decide. Then my sister was gone. Her friend asked me what I wanted to do about the date. I thought for a minute and then thought suddenly that possibly this girl would like to spend the evening with me. Just as I thought this, I remembered that I hadn't really noticed what she looked like. I asked her for a date just as she was walking away with her back turned. She turned around and I was happy to discover that she was attractive. She was THE GIRL WITH THE SPARKLING EYES. I asked her if she would talk with me, and she agreed. As she returned to me, I got up out of the gutter and walked away with her.

For purposes of the exercise with this dream, we have to assume that we have already been through the first step and made our associations, and some of them have "clicked." Now, in the second step, we have to apply those associations to specific dynamics in the inner life of this college student. Here are the connections that he could have made:*

---

*This is not an actual transcription of the work done by the dreamer. It was the first dream of his analysis and the work was mostly done during sessions with me. For purposes of illustration I've made a summary of connections that I recall were made or that legitimately could be made from the symbolism. I have put it in the first person to illustrate how a dreamer might write out the material on his own.

Second Step: What part of me, or what dynamic in my inner life, does each dream image refer to?

My grandmother's house	Since it is my maternal grandmother, and my mother was born there, this must be the "house of the Mother" inside me. It goes back generations, so it is perhaps more than just mother complex; it is the archetypal mother, the mother energy or mother presence inside my psyche. This is her territory, so it says that "I"—the ego—am in her territory. The ego is caught in the territory of the Great Mother, and in some way I am under her influence.

Now, where have I seen this functioning in my everyday life? There is a side of the mother principle, a regressive relationship that I can get into with it, where I start acting like a child who can't do anything for himself and just wants the world to take care of him. I feel dependent, I don't want to make decisions, I don't want to do anything for myself, and I just want someone to "mother" me. On this negative side, the mother energy has turned into a dependency complex. This is what I have seen in myself lately. I've given up my native masculinity, I'm afraid to venture out into the world and make my own way, I feel like I'm enveloped in the feminine side of myself, but in a negative way that makes me feel childlike and dependent.

Lying in the street	Where has this been going on in my life? I see it immediately. I have been depressed, in despair, unable to function at school, paralyzed, not knowing which way to turn. The image is an exact symbol of how I feel: like someone lying in the gutter, unable to get up, helpless. I feel that anyone can come

along and take a kick at me or run over me. I have no defenses and I can't help myself.

Another association that clicked is that this is a *public thoroughfare*. It is not my own space; it belongs to "them," out there. It seems that I am not only lost in the maternal feminine, I am also lost in collectivity. What do I find in my life that corresponds to that association? As I think about it, I realize that I have been revolving completely around what I think other people want me to do, or expect out of me. My going to college, the courses I took, the career plans, have basically come from some collective expectations that I assumed I had to live up to. I don't know whether they came from my family, from the society around me, or wherever—it scarcely matters. The point is that I have to start looking for the way of life that belongs to me, decide what values I want to serve, decide what is important to me, and start making my own decisions.

I think the only way I can get out of the street is to find the little plot of ground that really belongs to me, and stand there. I have to give up lying in the street and just stupidly accepting whatever collective notions come to me from the society around me.

My sister

If my sister in the dream represents a *person* living inside me, where is that inner person? Where do I have a feminine personality that is like my sister? One thing that "clicks" with me about my external sister is that whenever I am in a mood or depression she will act like this person in the dream. She tries to cheer me up, tries to draw me out of myself, tries to get me connected to the human race. Now that I look for it, I see that I have a feeling inside of me of wanting to connect up with people, wanting to find a friend I could be very close to. I don't want to be lonely.

Yet, I act just the way I act with the "sister" in the dream. I refuse to have anything to do with people; I act like a loner, preoccupied with my depression and my problems. I refuse relatedness. In the dream this is symbolized by my being unable to make a decision when she offers to set up a date. Maybe I don't want to get into dates, at this point, because I'm waiting for the Girl with the Sparkling Eyes, and don't know it. So I think my sister is the feminine force inside me that wants to draw me into relatedness with other people and with human life. But I can't seem to respond to that yet, because first I need to find my soul.

The girl with the sparkling eyes

I think of my ideal of the eternal feminine, the feminine presence I long for, as the "girl with the sparkling eyes." She feels somehow divine to me, like a princess or a goddess. When I see her, when I feel she is in my life, then I feel as though I am complete, as though I have something to live for, as though life has meaning. So she fits the description of the anima. She symbolizes my soul. This is the aspect of the feminine that, unlike the "sister," leads me toward the *inner* world, toward the spiritual world, toward inner experience and religious consciousness. She, my anima or soul, is the feminine presence inside me who wants an experience of God, who wants to explore the unconscious, wants to live in the world of dreams and archetypes.

The amazing thing is that, as soon as I see

who she is in the dream, I come out of my paralysis. I get up and I can walk. I start to live and function again.

Where do I see all this going on in my life? First, I have felt, in a manner of speaking, my soul longing for a different level of life. I came here, and started to learn how to look at my dreams, because I sense that there is an empty spot in me. I feel the need for an inner life, I feel an inner void, I want religious meaning, religious experience, or something that will give me a sense of the underlying meaning of my life. All of that going on inside me seems to be *her* presence: It is the Girl with the Sparkling Eyes, my soul, at work in me. These are her feelings that I am feeling. I have fantasies of a new, spiritual life, of delving deep into the mysteries of the unconscious. These must be *her* fantasies, coming out through my mind.

I asked her if she would talk with me

I asked her for a date, but it feels like the real turning point is when I ask her if she will talk with me. I am trying to set up a simple conversation, but it feels like the beginning of an exchange, a relationship.

Where do I find this going on inside me? As esoteric as it sounds, I think I am trying to find my soul, I am trying to set up a relationship to my own soul. Perhaps, in the moment that I decided I would write down my dream, and begin to look at dreams, start to live in the inner world—that was the moment when I said to my soul that I wanted to talk with her, that I wanted to get connected with my inner psyche and begin a friendship.

I got up out of the gutter

I can associate *getting up out of the gutter* with a very specific change inside me. As soon as I started understanding a little bit of this

dream, and started wanting to have an inner
life, I started feeling better. I don't feel as
helpless now. I don't feel paralyzed and at
the mercy of the world. I feel that there is
something that I can do to get life going
again, to understand what is going on inside
me. Opening up the inner world means that
hope and life force returns to me; I don't
have to lie in the gutter in passivity and
paralysis.

Our dreamer was able to connect his dream experience to some
very specific things going on in his emotional life. The dream was
amazingly on point for much of what he was feeling and experiencing. He felt absolutely helpless and defeated by life at that
time. The dream showed this vividly with the image of his lying in
the street, completely passive, utterly at the mercy of passersby.

This dream gives us a good example of a way in which archetypal amplification becomes helpful. In this case, it provides us with a
lot of information about the anima, so that we can see where she is
at work in his life. Once we see that the Girl with the Sparkling
Eyes is a soul-figure, a manifestation of anima, we can surmise several things. We know that anima leads us toward the inner world,
that she is primarily concerned with the inner life. From this we
can see that the meeting with this special person and the beginning of a relationship with her coincides with his decision to go to
the inner world, through his dreams, to renew his inner life. This
is, after all, the most direct way of going to anima and making relationship with her.

Step Three: Interpretations

The *interpretation* of your dream is the end result of all the work you have put into the earlier steps of dream work. The interpretation ties together all the meanings you have drawn from the dream into one, unified picture. It is a coherent statement of what the dream means to you as a whole.

At this stage you ask questions like: "What is the central, most important message that this dream is trying to communicate to me? What is it advising me to do? What is the overall meaning of the dream for my life?"

We don't have the right to make an interpretation of a dream until we have gone through the two earlier steps. Trying to make an interpretation without first making your individual associations is really just guesswork. If you take a ready-made interpretation out of a dream book, it is like wearing someone else's clothing that doesn't fit you. The interpretation should flow naturally out of the first two steps. The associations begin to tie together in your mind; the connections to your inner life become clear; and out of this is born a sense of the dream's overall meaning.

As part of your interpretation, you should try to make a simple statement of the one, main idea that the dream communicates. Ask yourself: "What is the single most important insight that the dream is trying to get across to me?"

Using the dream of the Girl with the Sparkling Eyes, I have prepared a sample interpretation to illustrate the kinds of ideas that might come out when you start to tie your dream together into an overall message.

As you read this example, remember that I had the advantage of working with the dream, years ago, and seeing what became of the dreamer in the aftermath of the dream, so the interpretation comes out of me a little more smoothly and coherently than it would if it were my own dream and I were trying to interpret it for the first time.

When you begin to interpret your dream, don't expect your in-

terpretation to come out in coherent form on the first try. Just
write down your ideas about how you think the entire dream fits
together and the meaning that it has for your life. Keep working
at it until it makes sense and fits with the overall pattern of events
in the dream.

I have put this example into the first person, as though the
dreamer were talking, for purposes of illustration.

Interpretation:
The Dream of the Girl with the Sparkling Eyes

What is the overall picture of my life that this dream brings to
me? The dream gives me a way to understand my emotional reactions, my depression and paralysis, and my inability to function at
school in the last several months.

I have been stuck in a severe neurosis. Since a neurosis is actually an unworkable gap between my conscious attitude and the
needs of my unconscious, I can see something of what has been
going on. My conscious attitude has been one of plowing ahead,
trying to succeed in college, and taking up the career that I now
feel was dictated to me by the world around me. But my inner being is demanding something quite opposite, which comes under
the heading of an *inner life*. That means meditation, working with
my dreams, finding out who I am, realizing that I have a soul—
just as humans used to believe, in the old religious sense, that they
had a part of themselves that connected them to God, and called
it the soul.

In the dream, the results of my trying to succeed in the collective world and stay in my dependent, mother complex is shown by
the image of my lying in the gutter, absolutely helpless, passive,
and dependent.

The dream shows me the three kinds of feminime energy inside
me that are active in my life right now. First, with the Great Mother, I have been caught in the negative side. I've gone completely
passive and dependent, and that has resulted in the terrible paralysis I've been in, my inability to function at school. But the other, even deeper, reason underlying all this is that I haven't been
living the life or pursuing the qualities that my deeper, inner self
is concerned with. I've been pursuing what I thought other people expected of me but not what my deepest instincts would lead

me to. So lying in the street in front of my maternal grandmother's house tells me that I'm caught in the mother complex in this regressive, childish sense, depending on others to tell me what to do and what to think.

Another side of the feminine at work in me is represented by my sister. This "earth feminine" wants to lead me back into relatedness to women and to the world at large. That is good, but I can't do it while I'm lying helpless in the mother complex and a collectively derived way of life. I have to learn how to relate to my inner self before I feel I can relate correctly to the people outside myself. Otherwise they seem to pull me into a collectivity that harms me rather than helps me.

The other feminine presence in me is the *Girl with the Sparkling Eyes*. I identify her as the image of my soul, my inner psyche, my anima. She is the force in me that pulls me toward the inner world, religious meaning, and the discovery of my own unconscious. She is like a goddess with sparkling eyes who could take me on the journey through the hidden world of my inner self, my soul, and show me how to live with who I am instead of what I think I ought to be.

How can I apply this information? First, I think that I have to give up, for a while, trying to be "somebody," trying to succeed in the academic world or the competitive world of success and power and social approval. Instead I need to do in my daily life what I do in the dream: Go off with my own soul for a while, and make it a journey of discovery into my own self.

I should take the time to dream, remember my dreams, work on my dreams, do inner work, try to find out what my deepest unconscious self wants of me, how it says I am to live. Then I think I can live without being in such terrible inner conflict and without winding up in the gutter again. According to this dream, to meet with my soul and explore my inner self is the only path open to me: That is the only thing that pulls me out of the gutter, puts strength into my legs, and enables me to stand up again like a man.

As you read over this interpretation you can see how it naturally grows out of the first and second steps of dream work that we have already gone through. By identifying which parts of his self are symbolized by the feminine figures in the dream and seeing where they have been affecting his life, he is ready to make an assessment of the dream's central message. It even leads to decisions about how to live his life in the future.

An adequate dream interpretation should sum up the meaning of your dream in a nutshell. It should also provide a specific application of the dream's message to your personal life, to what you are doing, to how you are going to live.

CHOOSING BETWEEN ALTERNATIVES

Sometimes you find that you can create several interpretations from your associations with the dream, and they all make sense. How do you decide among these possible interpretations? Sometimes you have one association with the symbol that is positive and encouraging, but another association that is negative, warning you that something isn't right. How do you decide which association is the right one?

Several approaches can help you to decide on the more likely interpretation. The most important technique is one that we have already learned: Write out your interpretations. When you write your interpretation on paper, it has a remarkable effect. It brings it off the level of fantasy and abstraction and gets it into a form that you can see clearly. With the act of writing, you begin to get a better feeling about whether it really makes sense to you or not. When it was spinning around in your head, it may have sounded fine to you. But when you write it down, you start seeing the holes in it; you see that it doesn't really correlate with the dream; it doesn't match what has been going on in your life. By writing it down, you see if it really hangs together, if it really "clicks."

DETERMINING ENERGY INTENSITY

Because your dream is composed of energy systems, a good test for an interpretation is whether it has energy behind it. If the interpretation arouses energy and strong feelings in you, if it suddenly gives you insights into your life, if you suddenly think of other areas of life where this interpretation makes sense, if it offers insights and liberates you from patterns you've been stuck in, all of these are signs that there is a tremendous energy behind this interpretation.

When you write out another interpretation, you are likely to find that it simply has no energy in it. It withers, it dies, you can't connect it to anything that has life or power for you. This is a good sign that the interpretation is not good for this dream.

FOLLOWING SMALL CLUES

In every mystery there is always a tiny clue, noticed only by the most observant, that leads to the solution. This literary ploy actually reflects an archetypal pattern in life and in dreams: Every dream provides us with some small detail, some small clue, that tells us which interpretation to follow, or how to take the dream.

Ten years ago a friend of mine was offered a job that sounded wonderful. He would start out as a full partner in the firm, would have challenging work, boundless opportunities. He was excited, but something told him to wait a couple of days before he made a decision. That same night he dreamed that a beautiful and voluptuous woman in a seductive evening gown walked toward him and let him know that she was his for the asking. He decided to go with her; but then she drew close, and he looked into her eyes. Her eyes were a strange, otherworldly shade of green that made him queasy and frightened him. He backed off.

The next day, the correlation between the seductive siren and the seductive employment offer was all too clear to him. He felt that he had projected his anima onto the new job possibility, but the dream was warning him that this was the witch aspect of anima. There was something inwardly wrong about the job offer, some hidden barb—so he refused it. He later found out, through other sources, that the firm was dishonest, and he realized that he could not have survived there.

He also found out about the archetypal meanings of the color green. Like every other color, green has both a positive and a negative connotation. When the color appears in nature—in trees and meadows—it is the symbol of the life force, the energy in nature that bursts forth in springtime. On the positive side, it symbolizes the renewal of life, but on the negative side, it represents *poison*—the venom in the snake, the pus in the wound, the secret venomous quality in the human race. One is said to be "green" with envy, for example.

The sickly, unfriendly shade of green in the eyes of the seductress was the clue, the special detail that told us how to interpret an ambiguous dream. A good job, a business opportunity—nothing wrong with that, on the surface. And a beautiful feminine figure approaching in your dream can be something excellent: the positive side of a woman's shadow, the appearance of a man's anima, a consciousness of the sensual and erotic, the opening up of one's feeling function. But if the shade of green in her eyes causes your hackles to rise, you have your clue.

Harold Goddard, the great Shakespearean scholar, has shown us that the principle is true in the plays of Shakespeare and perhaps in other great literature. The example that he gave, as I recall it, was the scene in *Romeo and Juliet* in which Juliet's father is discoursing on what kind of son-in-law he wants. He wants Juliet to marry someone who is rich and from another strong, wealthy family that would form an alliance with his own. All this sounds fairly normal and neutral for fifteenth-century Italy. It doesn't give us any terrible feeling about where the play is headed.

But then there is one detail, seemingly insignificant: the complaint of the maidservant. She says that the father's attitude is the same as selling Juliet into prostitution: He will sell her to the highest bidder, to the one who will bring in the most cash. The maid's statement gives us the small clue we need that things are not going well at a deep level in the destiny of this family. There is a deep split in its sense of values. Things are going badly, and the seeds of the tragedy ahead have already been planted.

In your own dreams, learn to watch for these small details and read what they are saying. They will make the difference in understanding a situation that would otherwise seem ambiguous.

ARGUING FROM OPPOSITES

If you find that the interpretation is still not coming clear, or you can't decide between the opposing interpretations, play devil's advocate with each explanation of the dream: Take sides, like an attorney, and argue strongly for each point of view, one at a time.

First, argue it affirmatively: Argue that it would be absolutely correct from an inner standpoint for you to take the job. Argue that it allows you to have the life-style that your dream prescribes for you. Argue that it would leave you plenty of time for your family, your inner work, and recreation. Gather all the evidence you can from your dream and list it.

The, argue the opposite position: Be the devil's advocate. Argue that the dream says you should stay where you are and maintain the status quo. Argue that you should put your energy into straightening out your inner life and healing your neurotic splits, rather than wasting your time getting into new jobs and new power plays. Argue the dream as a warning to not take the path or the direction that the dream seems to refer to. Argue first the *yin*, then the *yang*. Argue from the feminine instinct in you, then from your masculine side. Argue that you should leave it to fate and wait; then argue that you should take decisive action. By playing devil's advocate we force ourselves to align with each point of view within us, in its turn, until we see which one really reflects the lesson of this dream. You will usually find that there is some truth in both interpretations, and your final understanding will be a synthesis of different viewpoints.

Sometimes a dream says that there is no one "right" choice. You may take either path, and the dream tells you what the consequences will be for the one you choose. The dream tells you what price you will pay. The dream may be saying: "Look, here is the attitude you should take, but if you persist in the other attitude, here are the consequences that will follow."

The unconscious is fair with us. It allows our egos to do exactly what they insist on doing, so long as we take responsibility for our choices and accept the consequences. Even when we take the wrong turn, as we frequently do, we gain consciousness and learn from the experience—again, provided we accept responsibility for it and face the results honestly. Even something that seems "wrong" turns out to be of benefit if we are able to learn from it.

But the one thing that our unconscious will not tolerate is evasion of responsibility. The unconscious pushes us into one suffering after another, one impossible mess after another, until we are finally willing to wake up, see that it is we who are choosing these impossible paths, and take responsibility for our own decisions.

FOUR PRINCIPLES FOR VALIDATING INTERPRETATIONS

There are some general principles that you can refer to that will either confirm an interpretation or steer you away from one that is unsound. We will review four of them.

1. CHOOSE AN INTERPRETATION THAT SHOWS YOU SOMETHING YOU DIDN'T KNOW

Opt for the interpretation that teaches you something new, rather than one that seems to confirm your ingrained opinions and prejudices. Remember, the main function of a dream is to communicate something to you that you don't know, that you are unaware of, that lives in the unconscious. Your dream will not waste your time by telling you what you already know and understand; therefore, you should choose the interpretation that challenges your existing ideas rather than one that merely repeats what you already think you know.

There is one exception to this rule: Sometimes your dreams will send you the same basic message over and over again, but you either won't understand or won't put it into practice. In that case, the dream may *seem* to repeat something you already know. But if so, you had better begin to question why the dream has to keep repeating the message.

If dreams only served to affirm our pre-existing opinions and assumptions, they would not contribute to our psychological growth at all. Assume that your dream has come to challenge you, help you grow, wake you up to what you need to learn and where you need to change. And adjust your interpretation accordingly.

2. AVOID THE INTERPRETATION THAT INFLATES YOUR EGO OR IS SELF-CONGRATULATORY

Dreams often function as reporters. When you have made inner changes, straightened out your inner values, or made some advance on the path to maturity or individual development, they report back to you. You have a right to feel pleased when good things like these are reported to you.

However, dreams never report these things in a way that invites egotistical satisfaction. If you find yourself writing an interpretation of your dream that has you preening your feathers and congratulating yourself on how wonderful you are, how high above other mortals, then your interpretation is not accurate. Dreams don't give us those kinds of signals, and they don't invite us into ego inflations.

Dreams are aimed at the unfinished business of your life, showing what you need to face next, what you need to learn next. In the inner life, we never reach the point at which we can stop learning and start resting on our laurels. So if you find yourself writing a self-congratulatory interpretation of a particular dream, try to see it for what it is, understand that it can't be a very accurate reflection of your dream, and search further.

3. AVOID INTERPRETATIONS THAT SHIFT RESPONSIBILITY AWAY FROM YOURSELF

There is a strong temptation to use dreams to blame other people for the things that are going on in our lives. For example, if you have been feuding with someone at your job, and that person appears in your dream, it is all too convenient to say: "Good! My dream proves that I've been right all along. The other person is wrong, and the whole conflict is his fault, not mine."

This kind of interpretation is not only self-serving, it is usually completely inaccurate. Your dreams are not concerned with pointing out the faults of other people, or where other people need to change. You can leave that to the other person's dreams and the other person's own unconscious. You can leave that to God. Your dreams are concerned with *you*: what is going on inside you, the invisible energies that are shaping your inner path, the areas of your life where you need to become conscious or make changes.

If your dream comments on an external situation, it will focus on the contributions of *your* attitudes and unconscious behavior patterns.

4. LEARN TO LIVE WITH DREAMS OVER TIME—FIT THEM INTO THE LONG-TERM FLOW OF YOUR LIFE

Usually a dream can be understood in terms of specific events in your inner life in the last few days. Sometimes, however, you have a "big dream" that is showing you a panoramic view of your inner development over a long period of time. It may interpret for you what has happened in the past, show you what will take place in the future, and give you an idea of how your present experiences fit into that long-range flow. Sometimes it is hard to make a cut-and-dried interpretation of these dreams, because their full meaning only becomes clear with the passage of time.

We have to learn to live with dreams like these, and return to them regularly. As time goes by, our understanding increases. We see events in our lives, and suddenly realize that they fit exactly into the long-range developments that the dream spoke of. Such dreams are revealed as blueprints for our inner growth, and we learn, with time, to see how our lives match the blueprint.

If, after all your work, you can't honestly choose one definitive interpretation of your dream, then consent to live with it for a while. Be willing to live with the ambiguity of your dream just as we sometimes have to live with the ambiguity of life. You can legitimately say: "It may mean this, or it may mean that. It may go this way, or it might go another way. Only time will tell."

Such dreams come from the frontiers of your consciousness. They are joined in some way to the future, the seeds of which are contained already in you now. Give yourself time and experience, keep interacting with the symbols, return to the dream from time to time, and all will come clear.

Step Four: Rituals

By the time you reach this fourth step you have made an interpretation. You have done your best to understand the dream with your *mind*. Now it is time to do something *physical*. This step is very important because it helps you to integrate your dream experience into your conscious, waking life.

For some people this is a difficult stage of the dream work. When I ask, "What are you going to *do* about your dream?" they draw a blank. Yet, with a little practice, you learn to use your imagination and invent ingenious rituals that will give your dream immediacy and physical concreteness. You will be surprised at how much power this fourth step has to intensify your understanding of the dream, and even to change your habits and attitudes.

ACTING CONSCIOUSLY TO HONOR DREAMS

This step requires a *physical act* that will affirm the message of the dream. It could be a practical act: As a result of your dream, you may feel that you need to start paying your bills on time or straighten out a relationship that has become confused. Or it may be a symbolic act—a ritual that brings home the meaning of the dream in a powerful way.

Many examples come to mind. People sometimes dream that they need to be more aware of their feeling side, their feeling values. For such a dream you could make a ritual of spending one evening doing something that has deep value, that feels important and uplifting, but for which you never have time. Or do some small, subtle thing to show your affection to someone you care about. Small things work best: for example, dropping by for a short visit or sending a card. Any physical ritual will serve if it affirms the message of your dream.

If your dream tells you that you spend too much time on work, that you need more physical relaxation, you could make a ritual of taking yourself to the beach or some rural place, going for a long walk, focusing your eyes on the colors of earth and sky, reconnecting to the physical world. Even small acts like these have the power to make your dream concrete and to begin its integration into your conscious life.

One of the best rituals that I remember was done by a young college student who was analyzing with me. He dreamed that he was out in a shopping center on Saturday night. He went from place to place, and everything went badly for him. He found "junk food" that made him sick, superficial acquaintanceships, things to buy that left him unsatisfied.

He worked hard on the first three steps of his dream work. His interpretation was that the dream referred to his "Saturday night syndrome." This consisted of "going out with the guys," drinking a lot, eating unhealthy food, getting into adventures and acquaintanceships that felt empty afterwards. He decided, in light of his dream, that this kind of socializing or recreation was not healthy for him. It represented a set of values and a way of life that didn't belong to him.

I asked him: "What did you do about your dream? What was your fourth step?"

He decided that the essence of the dream was captured in the phrase, "junk food." In his dream he experienced the junk food of human relationship and collectivity. Like junk food, it gave him no nourishment in his inner life, his feeling life, or even in human relatedness. So he created this ritual for his dream:

He went to a hamburger stand and bought the biggest deluxe cheeseburger and an order of french fries. He got a shovel and took the junk food to his backyard. He dug a hole and buried the cheeseburger and fries with high, solemn ceremony. He did this as a symbolic act of renunciation. He ritually affirmed his intention to give up the superficial and destructive involvements that the dream had called to his attention.

This dream and this ritual had a profound effect on him. They initiated a great evolution in his consciousness, strength, and maturity. The ritual cured him of seeking nourishment where it could not be found, of giving his life over to people and activities that could not feed him on any deep level.

This is an instructive example of what our society does to our young people in general. We have lost the traditional forms of collectivity—the family, the clan, the school, the church—that would nourish them psychologically and spiritually. Most of the social forms and activities available to them do not contribute to their physical health or to their inner well-being. This general situation is well symbolized by the dream image of young people milling around a shopping center, aimlessly searching for something to do, someplace to go, a meaning or a connectedness that can't be found there. There is nothing inherently wrong with shopping centers. It is the shopping center *mentality*, shown in this young man's dream, that is the crux of the problem.

People are usually surprised to learn that the most powerful rituals are the small ones, the subtle ones. It is not necessary to do big things or expensive things. In fact, it is counterproductive to put out huge amounts of time or energy on your dream ritual. Don't set out to clean the entire house or try to whip your entire business into shape in one day because you had a dream that told you to get better organized. It is best that you not try to involve all your friends. You don't need to organize a jogging club and elect officers just because your dream told you to get more exercise.

Keep your physical rituals small and subtle, and they will be more powerful. The ritual is a physical representation of the inner attitude change that the dream called for, and it is this level of change that is requested by the dream.

It is also not a good idea to try to make a ritual out of talking about your dream or trying to explain yourself to people. Talking tends to put the whole experience back on an abstract level. It gets contaminated with your desire to present yourself in the best light. Instead of a vivid, private experience, you wind up with an amorphous, collective chat. The best rituals are physical, solitary, and silent: These are the ones that register most deeply with the unconscious.

USING THE BODY

Doing a physical act has a magical effect on dream work. It takes your understanding of the dream off the purely abstract level and gives it an immediate, concrete reality. It is a way of putting your dream into the here-and-now of your physical life.

Ritual and ceremony in general are ways of using small, symbolic acts to set up a connection between the conscious mind and the unconscious. Rituals provide us a way of taking principles from the unconscious and impressing them vividly on the conscious mind. But rituals also have an effect on the unconscious. A highly conscious ritual sends a powerful message back to the unconscious, causing changes to take place at the deep levels where our attitudes and values originate.

Once you have understood the meaning of your dream with your conscious mind, it is necessary to transplant your awareness and consciousness back into the deeper levels of the unconscious. We can think of this as taking a seed from a plant that has sprouted and replanting it back into the soil from which it grew. In the same way, when we replant our consciousness back into the unconscious, it produces new energy and new life below in the primal matter. The cycle of generation continues, and new forms push their way up to the level of consciousness.

Many years ago, when I was studying at the Jung Institute in Zurich, the famous Toni Wolffe (a colleague of Jung) was still working with patients there as an analyst. On this particular subject, doing something concrete about your dream, she was known as a holy terror. She met her patients at the door, and before they could even get into a chair, she would demand: "And what did you *do* about that dream from last week?"

Patients who had done something specific, something concrete and physical, were safe from the wrath to come. But if they hemmed and hawed, said they had thought about it a little, had talked with someone about it, or some such vague thing, she would turn them around and steer them back through the door. As the door was slamming behind them, she would say: "Come back when you mean business." That was the way it was with her, and everyone knew it: You either worked or you fled.

Toni Wolffe's idea was that dreams exist in modern people too much as airy thoughts, too much as abstractions in the head. One has to notify the rest of one's body that one has dreamed. She said: "People can analyze for twenty years, and nothing below the neck is aware that anything is going on! You have to do something about it. Do something with your muscles!"

Our tendency in the West is to make everything abstract, to use wordy discussion as a substitute for direct feeling experience. We have a tremendous need to get our bodies and our feelings involved. We have to transform our theoretical ideas into "gut-level" experience. Ideas and images from your dream should enter into your emotions, your muscle fibers, the cells of your body. It takes a physical act. When it registers physically, it also registers at the deepest levels of the psyche.

REDISCOVERING THE POWER OF RITUAL

Just as we have to overcome cultural prejudices in order to approach the unconscious, we also have to drop some of our ingrained prejudices in order to respect ritual as a necessary and helpful part of human life. Some of us automatically accept the idea that rituals are no more than remnants of a superstitious past or outdated religious beliefs. The words *ritual* and *ceremony* are often used disparagingly to mean "empty and meaningless formality."

In recent years, however, many people have become interested in shamanism and in the rituals of native American and other tribal cultures. We have begun to rediscover ritual as a natural human tool for connecting to our inner selves, focusing and refining our religious insights, and constellating psychological energy. We are beginning to learn that we have impoverished ourselves by giving up what our tribal ancestors had as part of their daily spiritual lives.

Jung anticipated this new awareness decades ago when he demonstrated that ritual and ceremony are important avenues to the unconscious: Ritual is a means of approaching the inner world that the human race evolved early in its history. The use of ritual goes back to the earliest dawn of time among our prehistoric ancestors. Ritual is one of the faculties we have, like dreaming, that enable us to set up a flow of communication between the conscious mind and the unconscious. Our instinctual hunger for meaningful ritual stays with us today, even though we have lost our sense of its psychological and spiritual role in our lives.

One of the meanings of the word *ceremony*, in its original Latin form, was "awe." A ceremony was a way of behaving when one

102 / DREAM WORK

felt a sense of awe or stood in awe. All the set formality around religious ceremony is an indication of the reverence and awe that people felt at one time regarding the object of the ceremony. It is natural for human beings to show reverence through formality, to use highly ritualized symbolic acts as a way to carefully approach the inner world.

How does this apply to dreams? When you have begun to experience your dreams, you sense that there is an enormous power and intelligence behind them. You feel that your dreams are revealing layers of your soul that you never knew, touching on themes that are so important that your whole sense of life and its meaning begins to be rearranged.

It is then that we need to know about ritual and its role in human life. Our religious lives are reawakened, we find ourselves facing the divine world, and we need ritual just as desperately as did the ancients before us. We need to make rituals in order to touch those dream energies and evolve them while at the same time maintaining our equilibrium in daily life. We need to express our awe and elation and gratitude—and sometimes, our terror. For all this, ritual is the channel that our instincts provide for us. In this, we are not different from our primordial ancestors.

All my experience as a psychologist leads me to the conclusion that a sense of *reverence* is necessary for psychological health. If a person has no sense of reverence, no feeling that there is anyone or anything that inspires awe, it generally indicates an ego inflation that cuts the conscious personality off completely from the nourishing springs of the unconscious. It is ironic, then, that so much of our modern culture is aimed at eradicating all reverence, all respect for the high truths and qualities that inspire a feeling of awe and worship in the human soul.

Ritual, in its true form, is one of the most meaningful channels for our awe and sense of worship. This is why ritual came spontaneously into being among humans in all parts of the earth. This is why modern people who are deprived of meaningful ritual feel a chronic sense of emptiness. They are denied contact with the great archetypes that nourish our soul-life.

If we look at ritual from a psychological standpoint, we may say that correct ritual is *symbolic behavior, consciously performed*. Different persons will have different language to express what is symbolized by the ritual acts. But the highest form of ritual has this characteristic: Those who participate sense that they are doing an act that has symbolic meaning, and they consciously seek to transform that act into an *active, dynamic symbol*. Their every movement becomes a symbol-in-motion that carries the power of the inner world into visible and physical form.

Whether we are aware of it or not, much of our behavior is symbolic. But what transforms physical acts into high ritual is the expression of symbolism within a *conscious* act. At its best, ritual is a series of physical acts that expresses in condensed form one's relationship to the inner world of the unconscious.

The role of ritual in the growth of consciousness is related to its power to make symbolic experience into something physical and concrete. Although we can understand the meaning of symbols with our minds, our understanding is made immeasurably deeper and more concrete when we *feel* the symbols with our bodies and our feelings. When we only think about symbols, or talk about them, we are able to detach ourselves too readily from the feeling quality that surrounds them. But if we *do* something to express the symbol—something that involves our bodies and our emotions—the symbol becomes a living reality for us. It etches itself indelibly on our consciousness.

Ritual is the tool that makes it possible to bring forth the essence of a dream situation, the essence of the principle the dream teaches, the essence of the archetypal energy in the dream; ritual reduces the voltage enough that we can translate them into immediate, concrete acts.

Without thinking about it in psychological terms, ancient and primitive cultures have always understood instinctively that ritual had a true function in their psychic lives. They understood ritual as a set of formal acts that brought them into immediate contact with the gods. Ritual served many purposes: It allowed them to show respect and reverence to the great Powers. It permitted them to touch the Power—the Power did not overwhelm them or possess them because the exchange was contained within the safe limits of ritual.

Like the burning bush that protected Moses' eyes from the sight of Jehovah, the animal forms of Zeus that shielded Semele from his horrible power (until she was so foolish as to demand to see him in his full godhead and was incinerated), the ritual protects the fragile ego consciousness of individual and tribe from the raw power of the unconscious. When ancient and primitive cultures spoke of "going to the gods" in their rituals, it meant in their archaic language that they approached the great and terrible archetypes of the collective unconscious.

In our time it is still the fashion to think of all this as naive and superstitious. But other cultures had a great advantage over us: They at least recognized the *existence* of the psychic realm, however they spoke of it, and learned to approach it through ritual and dream. By contrast, we modern people have mostly given up the language of religion. But few of us have found any other language for approaching the realm of the soul, and the terrible by-product of this is that we have forgotten its existence. In this respect we are worse off than our so-called primitive ancestors.

When we are learning to pay attention to our dreams and our inner world is the perfect time for us to rediscover the marvelous human faculty for ritual. There are no set rituals established for us, nothing that is prescribed by a formula or a tradition. Instead, each of us must go into our own imaginations and literally "dream" the ritual that will serve to honor a particular dream.

Each ritual must be custom-made out of the raw material of your own inner self. It flows out of the same inner place that produced your dream, your associations, and your interpretation. All inner work becomes much less threatening when we begin to see that every expression of the unconscious—whether dream, imagination, vision, or ritual—proceeds from the same reservoir deep within. And everything, therefore, works together.

THE CEREMONY OF THE FLOWERS

To illustrate ways that different people have custom-designed simple rituals to honor their dreams, we will look at a few more examples.

The first takes us back to a dream that we looked at earlier: the Dream of the Monastery. You may recall that I said earlier we would be returning to this dream to see what had happened with the dream and the dreamer when she approached the fourth step of dream work.

The dreamer's experience illustrates a fact that is well known to people who work regularly with their dreams: If we do our work inwardly and do small rituals to express our inner situation, it often generates a great charge of constructive energy in the external world around us and shapes our external circumstances in ways that we would never have anticipated. This is part of the evidence we have for the existence of the collective unconscious: We find that the unconscious connects us to other people and to our entire environment; therefore, when we focus a great deal of energy within the inner world, a parallel energy often arises in the people or situations around us. In this way we can do healing through our inner work that we never could have done through external means.

Here again is the Dream of the Monastery.

In the Monastery

I am in a monastic cloister, in a room or cell attached to the chapel. I am separated from the people and the rest of the chapel by a grille. Mass begins. I participate alone in my cell. I sit with crossed legs, *zazen* style, but holding my rosary. I hear the murmurs of the responses through the grille. The voices are tranquil. I close my eyes and I too receive communion, although no one and nothing physical enters my cell. The mass finishes. I become aware of flowers blooming at the side of my chamber. I feel a deep serenity.

After this woman worked on her dream, she saw the implications for her religious life and practice. But she couldn't think of anything *physical* to do about it. It seemed to be a matter of inner vision, of understanding inwardly. No outer act was implied: In fact, if she ran out and began searching for a religious group to join it would violate the spirit of the dream, which was to be quiet in her own awareness of the spirit.

Finally the young woman thought of a simple symbolic act she could do that would express her feelings about the dream and its meaning to her: In the dream, when she had received communion she saw that flowers had burst spontaneously into bloom at the side of her cell during the mass. She went and gathered flowers like those in her dream. She drove to the ocean with the flowers and made a solemn ceremony of going to the edge of the sea and casting the flowers into the waves.

She did this as a physical, yet symbolic, act of giving the gift she had received back to Mother Earth, back to the feminine sea of the unconscious. She felt at the time that this was too little, that she should think of something grander to do in honor of such a wonderful dream. But it was all she could think of, so she did it. She felt immensely grateful for the dream, and this was an act of gratitude toward God and toward the inner feminine.

Leaving the ocean, she drove quietly back to her house and found that a friend had come to visit while she was at the beach—a friend whom she did not see very often. Together they took a short drive around the neighborhood. Then several things occurred in rapid succession that seemed like coincidences, yet could not be.

First, as they drove, she discovered that there was a monastery in her neighborhood, just a few blocks from her home. She was startled, for inwardly she had been in a monastery all night and all morning. Her friend was one of the few laypeople who had permission to enter the cloister, and she even had a key for the gate! Her friend suggested that they stop and visit the chapel and greet the nuns.

When our dreamer walked into the monastery chapel, she felt as though she had walked back into her dream. The chapel, which she had never seen before, was identical to the chapel in her dream. Every detail was the same. She settled down by herself in the chapel to meditate in *zazen* posture, and all the meanings, feelings, and intense serenity of the dream experience flowed through her again.

In the days that followed she too was granted permission to visit the monastery regularly to meditate, spend quiet time, and nourish the part of her that is a monastic. The Dream of the Monastery became an external, physical reality as well as an inner reality in the Land of Dreaming. The inner flow and the outer flow became parallel energy systems moving in tandem.

The paradox in all this is that, at the point where she was ready to give up all external forms of "belonging" or of institutional religion, this woman suddenly found herself in a physical monastery, a physical chapel, a physical group of nuns with whom she can spend a few hours of her week in a sense of religious community. And none of this contradicts the inner monastery, the inner life of the spirit shown in her dream that is beyond external and collective religious forms.

As you can see, the ritual that the dreamer did for her great dream did not seem very dramatic to her. But her "ceremony of the flowers" was exactly appropriate to the simple and powerful symbols in the dream. It generated a connection between the inner world of the dream and the outer physical world, facilitated the synchronous events later in the day, and tied the two sides of her reality together.

If we learn to live this way, we find that all our dreams manifest both inwardly and outwardly. It is only our unawareness that prevents us from seeing the subtle connections. Our rituals and ceremonies can help us to see where the inner world and the physical world meet, and where they reflect each other as they move in parallel fields of energy.

WHEN YOU CAN'T THINK OF ANYTHING TO DO

You can always do a simple physical act, even if you can't think of something that relates directly to your dream. Go out and walk around the block in honor of your dream, if that is all you can think of. Light a candle. Do *something*. If you consciously do some act—any act—in honor of your dream, it will register with your unconscious.

I remember a marvelous man, a monk, who came to do analysis with me. He had never come closer to the incarnate world than Thomas Aquinas. He was an intellectual, and everything for him was spiritual, theoretical, and abstract. In response to his dreams he did the most airy flights in fantasy and theology. But his dreams never seemed to register with him in his emotional life, his practical life, his relationship to people or to the world around him.

Everything was fine until we came to the fourth stage of dream work. Then he would get angry with me. He didn't see why he should do anything about the dream. He thought it enough to understand with his mind, to grasp the theory.

One day we worked on a dream, and he got angry with me as usual and said, "So, what do you expect me to do about *this* one?" An irrational response jumped out of some place in my unconscious: "You could go out and look at the bark of ten trees in honor of the dream."

He looked at me, startled, stood up, muttered something, and backed out of the room. I felt a little sheepish. There wasn't anything about trees or bark in the dream. I was just as startled at what had come out of my mouth as he was.

About three hours later the monk came pounding on my door in high excitement. He said: "Robert! You don't know how interesting the bark on trees is! Some of it is brown; some is gray; some is smooth; some has great wrinkles in it. And little creatures live in it. It is a different color on the north side than on the south side, and moss grows on it, and . . . and you wouldn't believe how beautiful and interesting the bark on trees is!"

In that three hours, this man awakened for the first time to his physical being and to the physical world. He saw the spirit *in* the physical world, rather than dissociated from it. It was as though we had fashioned a Zen Buddhist *koan*: "What is the bark on ten trees?"

Koans are cryptic statements or vignettes that Zen *roshis* (masters) traditionally give to monks, ordering them to find the "answer" to the *koan*. But the *koan* is so constructed that no answer can be found within ordinary ego-logic. The monks must push themselves out of traditional categories and over the brink into irrational, intuitive wisdom. One famous example of a *koan* is this: Show me the sound of one hand clapping.

As with all *koans*, there can be no ordinary answer to the question, What is the bark on ten trees? But my friend discovered, as his answer, that you find the entire universe in the bark of ten trees!

USING COMMON SENSE

Your imagination will usually produce a good physical ritual for your dream. You should go to your imagination for help on this:

As we have learned, imagination and dreams come from the same source, and they are consonant. But not everything your imagination produces should be acted out externally. You still have to use your head!

The Hindu saint Sri Aurobindo once said, "Why is it that when people begin to relinquish the world, the first thing they relinquish is common sense?" You may feel as you confront the new and magical world of dreams that you are giving up your old, narrow world. But don't give up on common sense. Don't give up on courtesy or respect toward the people around you. This fourth step of dream work, this physical ritual, is a very powerful tool that can affect your life profoundly if it is used constructively. But if you use it in a silly or irresponsible way, it can cause you and other people a lot of grief. Think twice before you do things that are too dramatic or confrontational, that will involve other people and their feelings.

You should avoid doing things in response to your dreams that will get you unnecessarily into trouble. You should not get into destructive confrontations with other people. Don't use your dream as a license to act out.

Sometimes a dream will remind us of a conflict with another person. Or it may galvanize some longing in us to "break free from it all," to give up the restraints of society, responsibility, or commitment. In those situations you should be careful not to overreact, not to start rearranging your world or your relationships without giving it some long and careful thought. You can do a lot of damage if you go off "half-cocked."

Once I had a patient who was in graduate school. He was irritated with his roommate, a close friend, because his roommate was irresponsible. One night my patient dreamed that he gave his roommate an angry lecture and it ended in a fistfight.

When he awakened, his first impulse was to go and tell off his roommate, tell him what an ass he was, and have it out with him. But instead he did his dream work. He asked, "Who is the one *inside me* who is represented by my roommate's image?" He began to realize that he was really most upset with his *own* irresponsibility, which kept him from studying for his classes. He had chosen his friend's image to represent his own tendency to be lazy and disorganized.

When he came to the fourth step of dream work, he asked himself what physical ritual he could do to make his dream concrete. The temptation to go fight with his friend was still very strong, but he resisted it.

Instead, he sat down and wrote a long letter addressed to the part of himself that needed to grow up, make some decisions, and be an adult. He wrote several pages. He explained everything he had learned about taking responsibility, making choices and sacrifices, sticking to a schedule—everything that his *inner* "roommate" needed to know.

He put the letter in an envelope, addressed the envelope to himself, then went to the post office and made a formal ceremony of posting it. The next day the letter arrived in the mail. When he opened this envelope addressed to himself, he was shaken. It was as though the voice of the unconscious, coming from far away, was speaking to him through the letter. For weeks after that, he wrote a letter to himself every few days and mailed it to himself. With each letter that he received, the message and the implications of his dream burned themselves more deeply into his consciousness. It permanently altered his view of his life.

This example illustrates our principle: The fourth step of dream work does not consist in dramatically confronting people you are angry with, breaking up relationships, or doing destructive things. It does not consist of trying to "straighten things out" with a lot of talk. That leads nowhere. It should be a physical ritual that affirms your own personal responsibility for your dream and for the issue it portrays.

If you do have unfinished business with some external person, you will be able to approach it in a constructive and noncombative way after you have done your dream work, done your private ritual, taken responsibility for your share of the confusion.

Keep your rituals subtle and low-key, positive and affirmative, and you will get the best from them.

Ritual is one of our most powerful tools for making a synthesis between the polarities of human reality. It is an art that ties our two halves together. The archetypal, spiritual *yang* needs to be tied to the here-and-now earthiness of our *yin* nature. The masculine spirit, that gets so lost in abstraction and theory, needs to be anchored to the feminine earth, needs to experience directly the feminine soul. The path to the feminine side of reality is through concreteness, matter as *mater* (mother), earth-connectedness. All of this constellates most directly through the physical act.

The world you see in your dream is the inner world that exists outside time and space. Some of its energy and its message must be *incarnated* into this human world of the here-and-now. It must find its way into your daily life, for its truth is lost unless you live it.

DREAM WORK ILLUSTRATION: THE FOUR HOODLUMS

To illustrate our four-step system in a practical way, I am going to work through a sample dream, and you are invited to join me. This is a fairly short dream that I had many years ago. But dreams that seem small and simple can have earth-shaking implications for the dreamer, as this one did for me. This dream also illustrates how archetypal references can be used in combination with purely personal associations to produce a sense of the dream's message.

Here is my dream.

The Dream of the Four Hoodlums

I am in my hometown, Portland, Oregon. I am walking on Williams Avenue, the street I used to walk down to get to grammar school. This is my old neighborhood, just as it was in the days of my childhood. I walk past the Japanese greengrocer's on the corner, and the store is still there. It seems that I am visiting the old neighborhood. I feel that I am my present age, but I've been transported back to that place as it once was.

I walk past a vacant lot. I feel that there is something lurking there. I have a sudden intuition that I will be robbed. I stop and take my wallet out of my hip pocket and remove the cash. I see that I have forty dollars. I slip the cash into my left shirt pocket, over my chest, and put the wallet back into my hip pocket.

Four young hoodlums jump out of the shrubbery and surround me. I know that this is the robbery I intuited. I see it is useless to run: There are four of them; they are younger and stronger than I. They are "street people" and can easily overpower me.

They search me carefully, starting at my shoes and working upward. When they reach my hip pockets, they find my wallet but no money, so they keep searching. When they get to my shirt pocket on the left side, they find the forty dollars. But, by that time, they have spent so much time with me and there has been so much physical touching that they "know me." In a sense we have become acquainted, become friends.

They stay, talking with me in a friendly way, but they don't take my money, because now we are friends, and you don't take your friends' money. I feel absurdly happy to have these hoodlums as friends and like them very much.

STEP ONE: MAKING THE ASSOCIATIONS

As we go through the dream, I am going to use two formats to illustrate two ways that you can lay out your associations on paper. The first format is very concise and abbreviated. As you see below, I put the symbol in the left margin, and then write down, in the most abbreviated form, whatever associations come out of my mind in response to the symbol.

The second format is more a conversational way of talking to yourself on paper about your associations. I will also use the second format as an informal commentary for the reader, explaining how I came up with some of my associations. You may use either of these formats, or use the "wheel and spokes" method of diagraming that we learned earlier.

As you read through this material, you will notice that I usually have a lot of associations with every image, and only a few of those associations really turn out to "click" or fit into the final interpretation. In fact, you might find yourself getting impatient with all this meandering, page after page, through associations that don't turn out to be applicable in the end.

I have deliberately left in all these associations so that you can see what a person actually has to go through in order to try out all the different associations, find the ones that "click," fit them to inner parts of the self, and finally weld everything together into an interpretation. It took me a couple of weeks of returning to this dream and coming up with associations before it all started to fall into place. But it was worth it: The dream altered my conception of who I am and changed the course of my life.

My Associations to the Dream Symbols

Williams Avenue and the old neighborhood

Time of childhood before waking up to conflict: "Garden of Eden." Streets: First place child aware of people congregating, collectivity. Beginning of collective existence. Nostalgia.

Williams Avenue represents to me that time of life when I was a child, before I "woke up" and became aware of the divisions and conflicts inherent in life. Childhood in that neighborhood, with its old wooden houses, was a simple, happy time. Williams Avenue is, for me, *the* street: the archetypal street that formed my whole feeling of streets as places where people live and congregate, where there are businesses, little hubs of civilization and human collective existence. I was in a "Garden of Eden" in that neighborhood. It was before I woke up to ethical conflicts, right and wrong, before I learned there was betrayal and hatred in the world. It is my preconscious Garden of Eden.

The Japanese greengrocer

People of another culture. Culture with ritual, ceremony, grace, delicacy. Lady in kimono. Courtesy. Basket of lilacs, rice cakes. Zen Buddhism. India. Feeling and relatedness. Relationship outside of projection, casualness, sentimentality.

The first thing that comes to mind is that this was my first experience of meeting people of another culture, and they fascinated me. I became aware, for the first time, of the differences in people, aware of a way of doing things that was ritualized, graceful, delicate. I remember that a relative arrived from Japan, dressed in a kimono. There was bowing and exchanging of courtesies while I looked on, struck with the beauty of the formalities, the courtesy and respect that old-fashioned Japanese people knew how to show, something I'd never seen in middle-class Portland among my own Anglo tribe.

The Japanese family brought out a little bit of the sense of courtesy and formality in my own family: Each year my grandmother sent a basket of lilacs to them, and a day later a package of delicate rice cakes was always delivered to our house as a return gift.

The world that the Japanese greengrocer opened up in me is a vision that I have been trying instinctively to augment ever since. It was the beginning of the impulse that led me to travel to Japan and India. I associate it with my spontaneous interest in Zen Buddhism, Eastern philosophy, Hindu culture. The Japanese family constellated a sense in me of something high, noble, and beautiful that was outside my own cultural experience.

Years later I understood that traditional Eastern people also represented to me a capacity for warmth and relatedness that is not the same as "getting personal" in the shallow, casual, artificial, back-slapping way that so many Americans use as a substitute for genuine feeling and relatedness. And Japanese culture, especially the Zen culture, represents, at its best, a true respect for the inner world, for religious experience, and for beauty. All these associations come to mind from this one symbol.

The vacant lot

Undeveloped = primitive, wild place in middle of city. Bounded by streets = limits, boundaries, form, structure. But no form in vacant lot. Uncivilized. Outside reach of law. Piece of wilderness. Have to clear weeds annually, fire hazard. Hiding place for outlaws.

Retreat. Religious retreat? Shadowy place: Place of shadow? Unconscious place in the middle of conscious areas?

To me, a vacant lot is a piece of untouched, primitive land in the middle of the city. Everything around it is civilized, developed, turned to human use, but the lot is still like a piece of wilderness. Although the vacant lot is bounded and defined by streets (which I think represent "civilization" to me), it is not "civilized." It feels like a place that is "outside the law," like the Sherwood Forest of Robin Hood, where the hoodlums, literally "out-laws," could lurk. I also associate it with unconsciousness and with the shadow: a place inside me that is circumscribed by consciousness but is in the shadow and outside my conscious control.

Wallet

Place where you keep money, so place for keeping resources. Credit cards, ID, therefore wallet = a kind of *passport* for getting by with people. Wallet usually goes at hip pocket, keeps money at "hip" level. Wallet = useful, but can also be for show; pretentious, an artificial form of security.

The money

Forty dollars = four. Four = wholeness, completeness, totality, the completion of a cycle or synthesis. Money is a resource. Energy? Power? Psychological strength or power. Life force. Something you invest. Keep it at the "hip" level or at the chest level. Where is it invested? Where is it put to work?

This is where archetypal amplification begins to help. I know that numbers are very important in dreams, and I know that the number four is a traditional symbol of completeness, unity, wholeness, totality. This is so in most religions, in alchemy, in ancient philosophical systems. The Greeks believed in four elements (earth, air, fire, and water). The Christian mandala has twelve disciples grouped in four sections around Christ. The American Indians structured their religions around four directions and four winds. It represents a bringing together of the main elements of the individual into a whole consciousness.

Money seems to be associated with *resources*: perhaps physical or psychological energy or, at a deeper level, life force. Money is something one *invests*. So where am I investing my life force, my attention, my main energy? Resources are also personal talents, strengths, intelligence. You can use money to get something done: thus, a capacity for practical things, getting something accomplished. Money is something we *earn* by our efforts. It represents the accumulated value of our work, discipline, expertise.

The hip pocket

One of the *chakras* [centers of consciousness] is close to hips, the visceral, emotional side of the personality, center that controls visceral energies. To be "hip"—opium user. Origin of "hippie" = originally, into drug scene. Also hip = to be "into the scene," "hip" to what is going on, "hip to the jive."

I learned that the phrase *to be hip* came from the old opium subculture, where to be "on your hip" meant to lie in an opium trance. When psychedelic drugs and marijuana became popular among the Beat generation, people who were into such things were "hip." From this came the slang "hippie." What are my associations? Most of "hippie" life to me represents a pretense of going into a life of "love" and "spirituality" while actually being irresponsible and dependent. It is a way of staying in the negative side of the mother complex.

Another association: "shooting from the hip."

In kundalini yoga there is a *chakra* located in the region of the hips, a center of consciousness. I think it controls the *visceral* energies, which in yogic symbolism means the raw emotions and raw, instinctual animal energies. After one has developed that center of consciousness, the consciousness has to be moved up to the higher *chakras* in the body, so moving my money away from the hip up to the chest level could mean moving the focus of my life away from the visceral or "hip" level.

The other association that clicks for me is the idea of being "hip" in the sense of "with it" or "into the scene." I can think of examples of my investing my energy in trying to be "in" with a group of people, or connected, so that I would feel "part of the scene."

Left shirt pocket over chest

Over heart. Heart level. Heart values = feeling values. Feeling function. *Anahata chakra* in kundalini. Invest energy at heart level. Feeling relationships to people.

This dream was like a mystery story that slowly unfolded for me. At first I could not make any associations to the left shirt pocket. I sensed that the movement of the forty dollars up to that pocket was somehow the crucial point in the dream, the one that produced all the rest of the events. But I could not for the life of me find an association that really "clicked" for me.

I don't know how long it was—days, perhaps weeks—that I tried all sorts of crazy associations. Then it occurred to me that the pocket was over the heart, or at the level of the heart. If the pants pocket could be called the "hip" pocket, this shirt pocket could as well be called the "heart" pocket. That opened up a flood of associations. Heart values are *feeling* values. The heart level is the feeling level.

In Jung's model, the feeling function is not connected with emotions, as some people assume. Feelings and emotions are distinct energy systems in the psyche. When people *feel*, they are actually assigning value. If you feel love toward another person, you are assigning the highest value to that person, affirming that person's worth, value. When you *feel* that something is beautiful, you are again assigning a value or recognizing a value in that thing.

Therefore the feeling function could better be called the *valuing* function. It is the function in the psyche that has the job of recognizing values in people, things, and ideas and distinguishing what has high value from what has low value. It is your feeling function that tells you whether certain people are good for you, "nourishing" for you, in a feeling sense, or poisonous for you. If your feeling function is working consciously, it tells you what is right for you and what would be destructive for you.

Once I saw that the shirt pocket corresponded to the *heart* level, further associations with kundalini yoga were opened up. The *anahata chakra* also is located at the level of the heart. This center of consciousness is reputed to generate and control the refined feelings: the powers of love, refined discrimination in feeling matters, appreciation of beauty, spiritual feeling, unselfish love, and relatedness toward other people. This *chakra* generates the feelings about what is good, true, noble, or beautiful. Kundalini makes the same distinction between feelings and emotions, apparently, for the raw, primitive emotions, that which makes one an "emotional" or volatile person, are associated with a lower *chakra*, while only the more refined and "rational" feelings proceed from the *anahata chakra*.

The hoodlums

Outlaws. People outside the "law" = something outside the established "order" of the conscious mind or my ego world. Outside what society has decreed. Shadow. Saboteurs, because they steal money, therefore steal my energy, power, resources. *Four* hoodlums = affinity with the fourness of the forty dollars. *Four* = completeness, unity, wholeness. Wholeness comes through the "hoodlum" side of my psyche? They steal my energy unless I put it at the heart level? *Gang* = "gang up on me."

As you can see, my mind is already trying to skip to the second step of the dream work: I am spontaneously thinking about what part of my interior self these hoodlums are. I associate them with the *shadow*, because they seem to live within the ego's general "field of consciousness," that is, the civilized town, but they live in a shadowy, unconscious vacant lot, outside my consciousness or control. They are unconscious, apparently repressed, parts of my masculine side that are trying to be assimilated into the conscious ego or make a synthesis with it.

Since they are "outlaws," this means to me that they are outside the control of my ego's established world, outside my established attitudes or my self-image, my concept of myself.

There are *four*. This tells me that, paradoxically, although they are hoodlums and muggers, they represent *wholeness* for me. That means I have to bring them into my conscious life in order to complete the self and be a total individual.

I associate the *robbery* with a basic psychological principle: If you repress a part of yourself and keep it out of your conscious life, it turns into a robber and starts "stealing" your time and energy by creating a neurosis. This is its way of trying to force its way into your life. It sabotages you and prevents you from functioning as you want to. The "robbery" can take the form of physical symptoms, illness, neurosis, anxiety, or even "bad luck" that seems to "gang up on you" just as the four hoodlums do in this dream.

I associate the *overpowering* of my ego in the dream with the fact that the archetypes of the unconscious generally have more power than the ego. If my ego refuses to make a synthesis with the unconscious contents, the unconscious has the power to bring my ego-life to a standstill. I am brought to a halt in the dream, and if the situation were not mended in a positive way, later I would experience that "halt" in my practical life.

Search for
the money

Physical contact in dreams means communication between parts of psyche. Communication between polarities: conscious–unconscious, ego–"hoodlums," ego–shadow. Synthesis in psyche starts as conflict, ends in friendship. Search for resources. Finding money not as important as finding where I put it.

Friends,
becoming friends

Ending conflict, joining forces, joining pairs of opposites: respectable ego with primitive hoodlums. Synthesis with other part of self. Synthesis with shadow. Go over to shadow's point of view. Communication begins in conflict, stealing. Ends in synthesis or partnership. Learn from hoodlum. Make room for lawlessness in life. Friendship possible if money invested at right level.

All the interactions we see between the persons in our dreams are forms of communication among the various parts of our total self. There may be fighting, wars, love, hate, friendship, enmity—all this is a kind of rubbing together of the polarities, a "getting acquainted" among the different energy systems that coexist within us.

So this searching for the money, in a curious way, is the one form of communication my ego has with the "hoodlum," shadow, part of myself. Most communication in the psyche begins in conflict. The unconscious parts of our personalities have to fight for "equal time," for some recognition, against the dominant attitudes and power systems of the conscious mind. But fighting, robbing, some kind of confrontation, is better than no contact at all. If, from the conflict, the ego can learn to open itself to the viewpoints and values of the shadow side, then the conflict slowly evolves into friendship and synthesis.

STEP TWO: APPLYING THE DREAM IMAGES TO SPECIFIC PARTS OF MYSELF AND DYNAMICS IN MY INNER LIFE

Williams Avenue

I am trying now to find the part of myself, and the actual dynamics going on inside myself, that Williams Avenue represents.

One association that clicked was the Garden of Eden: that is, it is the original, unsplit, childhood state in which one feels no division of the world. One feels completely unified with parents, family, the world around. There are no discordant issues to deal with, no conflicts.

Why would this come up in this dream? What goes on inside me that this fits into? When something of childhood comes up, that may be a sign that the dream is talking about the overall picture of one's life, the progression or developmental stages that have gone on since childhood up to the present. So, I could look for a passage from one developmental stage to another.

The clue, here, is the Japanese greengrocer. How do I contrast the quality of the Japanese family with the quality of Williams Avenue in general? If I look at this as stages and influences, it falls into place: Williams Avenue is my basic orientation to the world, as a child, in my white, middle-class, extroverted, sensation-oriented attitude.

The foreign element in my own personality that was going to come into conflict inevitably with my childhood Anglo world, is represented by the Japanese family on the corner: it is the introverted, feeling side of me, the heart quality in me, a different set of values than my Anglo culture had.

Dreams are said to have four stages of development, all of which must be present to make a complete dream:

1. *Dramatis personae* (persons and places)
2. Statement of the problem
3. Response to the problem within the dream (development)
4. *Lysis* (i.e., outcome, or resolution)

The original setting is Williams Avenue, which is my set, tight, extroverted, practical

Anglo world. The problem is stated when I see the Japanese greengrocer's. The problem is an encounter, starting in early childhood, with a culture that represents opposing values. But all that culture does is awaken the child to the opposing values that were already sleeping within him, dormant, waiting to be awakened. This is the beginning of a lifelong encounter with the shadow, a movement toward completing the self.

The response to this problem, the development of this theme, comes later with the relocation of the forty dollars to the heart level and the robbery by the four hoodlums.

So, in order to be a little more specific, if I ask what part of me Williams Avenue is, I can say that it is the seed of my present ego structure, the beginnings of the value system that later became my dominant attitude and main viewpoint toward life. What is important to this dream is that this dominant attitude is one that squelches feeling, that is embarrassed by feeling and equates it with embarrassing emotionalism. It is a culture that mostly uses sentimentality as a substitute for real feeling.

The Japanese greengrocer

It is as though I have a separate little "civilization" living inside me that is like the old-fashioned Zen Buddhist culture of Japan. That part of me is focused on inner things, on the life of the soul, on contemplating the archetypes and the face of God, searching for inner harmony and consciousness. Even the external things that my inner Japanese culture is concerned with—the beauty of a kimono, the delicate formalities and courtesies in relationships, the graceful ways of showing respect and doing things—all are outward symbols of the harmony of the inner realm that one works for. They too refer me back to the divine world. They strike me as "outward signs of an inner grace."

The world I was born into on Williams Avenue taught me to be concerned mostly with outer things: Make a decent living, get the bills paid, get things done, get the house built and the garden planted, get along with the neighbors, and stay respectable in the eyes of the townsfolk. These qualities have their own value and relevance in life, but there is little room for the inner world in them.

It is the "Japanese" part of me that is interested in medieval, archetypal Christianity, in Zen, Hinduism, the great myths. It is the part of me that finds high, noble, and beautiful qualities in other cultures and religions.

But my main association is to the introverted, feeling quality in me. It corresponds later in the dream to the "heart" level. It is a capacity for relationship that, at its best, does not get sentimental or "personal" in the sense of casual and artificial. It values loyalty and substance in relationships rather than effusive words or shows of emotion that don't last.

The vacant lot

This seems to be a "place" inside my psyche that is surrounded by my ego structure or conscious mind (city streets) but is a little piece of unconscious wilderness, outside the control of my ego, where nature has its way and my shadow can hide out.

Can I find anything specific in my life that seems to correspond to this place? I know that there are funny "places" in my personality, lapses or lacunae, where I am suddenly uncivilized, without warning. It is as though I had suddenly reverted to the forest or jungle. They embarrass me, and I try to control them, but often I am unsuccessful.

I have been learning, however, that sometimes these are the areas in me where there is more spontaneity, life, feeling, and natural humanness than anywhere else. By trying to bring all these "vacant lots" under regimented control and make them respectable, I often squelch the best or most natural parts of myself.

I try to wade into these areas of my personality periodically—much as the fire department comes and cleans out the dead grass to reduce the fire hazard—to a little bit of consciousness and civilization there. But otherwise I decide to let the weeds and wildflowers grow unmolested.

I relate this to my feeling side. I get sudden enthusiasms for people. I suddenly like certain people and want to do things for them or spend time with them. I suddenly come off my formal, restrained, "civilized," English gentleman persona and pour out my love or appreciation to someone in a spontaneous burst of enthusiasm. I often feel embarrassed by this and fear that I've embarrassed other people or that things are "out of control." But this quality often reaches out of me and starts warm, good friendships. It has led me into deep, satisfying relationships with people in many different lands and cultures.

I am often in a quandary over this "vacant lot" inside me. I keep thinking I should clean it up, develop it, get it under control. But then I conclude that it is better to let nature run it. Sometimes, in the areas of love and feeling, wild grasses and wildflowers are better than formal gardens.

The wallet and the money

Based on my associations, I think the money refers to my inner resources, my main energy and life force. The dream is focused on the question of where I focus my energy and my life. Money is something you invest, so where do I invest the main strength and resources, the main purpose and meaning of my life? In colloquial terms, where do I "bet my money"? Do I "put my money where my mouth is"?

The *fourness* of the money tells me this is no minor issue. This is my main life energy, the principle thrust or direction or commitment of my life. Where I put this dream money is symbolically the place where I invest my entire self, my life, my highest capacities. What values, what aspect of life am I committing all of that to?

The hip pocket

I am connecting this image to several overlapping collective attitude systems or beliefs inside me, a basic, unconscious, assumed way of looking at things. First, it is an attitude of wanting to be "hip" in the sense of being included in what certain groups of people are doing, wanting to be in or part of "the scene." Also, I associate it with the "hippie" pattern of talking about "peace" and "love" when actually other motives are lurking behind the sentimental verbiage. All this adds up to a kind of collective *imitation* of deep feeling, but it is really a way of talking the language in order to fit in with people or with a fad. So I think the movement of my money away from that level and up to the heart level tells me that I have to move the money away from collective expressions of emotion or sentimentality and invest myself in real feeling relatedness to individuals and to the values that genuinely mean something to me.

Shirt pocket over left side of chest

In the first step, two ideas "clicked" strongly for me. One is the heart, and heart values. Second is the *anahata chakra* in kundalini yoga. Either way, I am connecting all this to the feeling function inside me and the feeling life within.

In step one I explained something of the feeling function and the difference between emotions and feelings. It took me a long time to come to the point where I associated this detail, the left shirt pocket, with the feeling side of myself. This is because I had never thought of myself as a *feeling* kind of person. I thought "feeling types" were the highly emotional ones. I thought that, since I'm not given to displays of emotion and can't stand much sentimentality, I was not a feeling type, that I was dominated by thinking or intuition.

It was this association to the heart that made me look more closely and see that Jung did not mean "emotional" when he referred to a *feeling* type or a *feeling* function. This symbol forced me to look more closely at myself. I began to realize that the aspect of life that really motivates me, around which I involuntarily revolve my life, is the feeling side: the people who draw my love and whose magnificent quality I sense, and the values that capture my devotion and loyalty. It is these feeling relationships, of valuing and sensing the value in people, that energize my life and give it its center. That which moves me and inspires me most deeply in all of life is the beauty, nobility, and inner quality that I see in the human beings who come in contact with me.

Until I had this dream, I had always tried to repress this stream of energy in me, downplay it and keep it under wraps. In the family and the culture in which I grew up, feeling was not openly displayed. It was considered embarrassing, untrustworthy, impractical. If you were moved too deeply by a symphony, you would be considered a little strange. If you showed too much affection, it made others uncomfortable. Anyone who made decisions from the heart, rather than from cool practicality, was considered suspect as undependable. To feel, to love intensely, to be intoxicated with the beauty of a person, something in nature, or a value—all this would be inappropriate and out of place in respectable society.

In the aftermath of this dream, and my interaction with this symbol, I discovered my typology and the laws that go with it—I find that I am an introverted, feeling type, and the mainspring of my life is different than I had thought. So, I identified the part of myself that seems to correspond to this symbol—and I found a specific set of dynamics in my inner life that showed this part of me in action.

The movement of the money to this pocket seemed to me to represent a new investment of my energy, my capacities, my life itself, in the feeling function. I felt that it represented investing in a new center of consciousness, corresponding to the heart and the *anahata chakra*.

The hoodlums

During the first step I said that I associate the hoodlums with my inner *shadow*, my alter ego that is still unconscious and contains aspects of my personality that have yet to be integrated into my ego's point of view. And I have to find specific aspects of my life in which I see this shadow at work.

If I look at my dream, again, as a series of developmental stages, something comes clear. The hoodlum side seems to be a reappearance of the *other* complication in my Williams Avenue background: the Japanese greengrocer. The problem is the appearance of an *introverted, feeling quality* in my life, setting up a terrible conflict with my Anglo culture and training. It shows up first in the Japanese family. Then it reappears, and the conflict goes into a further development in the form of the shadow, the hoodlum quality.

The introverted, feeling quality is mine. But it couldn't find a respectable place to live in my ego world. Therefore it got repressed into a vacant lot, a little island of the unconscious inside my field of consciousness. My ego sees this part of me as a "hoodlum," but since the hoodlum appears as *four*, the dream is telling me that the hoodlum is a crucial part of me and that I need him in order to make myself whole.

Another reason that these shadow parts of ourselves show up as "hoodlums" is that they are forced into a "life of crime," so to speak, in order to survive in a world that is dominated by the ego and the ego's values. For example, if a feeling kind of man refuses to live his feeling side, his shadow will steal energy from him and invest it for him in his feeling side. Mostly this is done by compulsions: We fall in love against our will. Our hearts suddenly go off on crazy paths of their own, leaving our cool, collected minds aghast and struggling vainly to maintain order and dignity.

Our hoodlum feelings also steal energy by putting us into depressions and other moods. They make us physically ill. Depressions and moods and illness produce rather low-grade feeling lives, but the unconscious apparently feels that something is better than nothing. But our inner hoodlums also perform a noble role: Like Robin Hood, they steal from the rich and give to the poor. They steal from our wealthy ego empires and give to our undernourished feeling functions.

I could see this part of myself at work in my life in another way, also: The dream showed that the conflict between me and my hoodlum shadow went on and on until finally we became friends. And the crucial thing I had to do in order to stop the robbery, the loss of energy, and to become friends was to relocate my money at a different level—at the heart level. I could see that I had been in this conflict with my introverted, feeling side for many years, and it had been robbing me, through compulsions, through depressions, through psychosomatic illness. And finally, now, I could see that it was possible for me to put my money at the heart level, acknowledge my true feeling nature, and make friends with my hoodlums.

AN INTERPRETATION

As you may have noticed, I got somewhat carried away during the second step of my dream work, and I wound up doing a lot of the actual *interpretation*—developing an overview of the dream, seeing the dream in developmental stages, tying the dream together—that should actually be part of the *interpretation* stage. Sometimes it happens that way. You get halfway through the first step or the second step, and something lights up inside you, and you start tying the whole dream together. Fine. It doesn't really matter when the overall interpretation starts pouring out of you, as long as it gets done.

As a result, my interpretation can perhaps be rather short and to the point. I can go directly to the question of "What is the main, overall meaning that this dream has for me and my life?"

Primarily, the dream shows me that I am someone different than I thought I was, and that I have the *right*, as well as the duty, to live in accord with who I really am. In the aftermath of the dream I discover that I am an introverted, feeling type. The main focus of my life has to be my feeling values and my feeling relationships to the world around me, but especially to people.

Now, what does this mean to me, in practice, in the way I live my life? I can take courage and start devoting myself consciously, deliberately, to the feeling world. I can devote a large portion of my time and energy to cultivating my friendships, my relationships with people. I can devote time to the activities and subjects that have quality and depth and profound meaning for me. Most important, I can do this without feeling guilty, without feeling that I am giving in to some "hoodlum" side of myself, entertaining myself with the warm companionship of human beings when I ought to be doing something "useful."

The essence of this dream is the relocation of energy: the relocation of energy from other levels to the "heart" level, the feeling level, of life. I don't have to spend my life trying to think, be logical and intellectual.

The dream shows this to me in a perspective that takes into account my entire life and a slow evolution that has gone on throughout my life up until the time of the dream. That evolution begins with childhood in the "Garden of Eden," where I assume that there is only one viewpoint in life, that of my middle-class, Anglo Portland family and neighborhood. This becomes the dominant attitude system, the attitude system that runs my life for years to come, that defines my social personality and my concept of myself.

The "problem" aspect of the evolution—the conflict that must come into every life in order to engender growth—is symbolized to me as a child by the presence of the Japanese family, examples of an introverted, feeling culture that contrasts with my own and sets up involuntary resonances in the secret places in my soul. That urge, to be, in the midst of an unfeeling culture, a feeling human being, becomes the "hoodlum" in my unconscious, banished to the vacant lot, kept in hiding.

The *lysis* (resolution) of the dream, the resolution of the conflict, the healing of the split in the psyche, takes the form of this *relocation of energy* that is symbolized by the placing of my money at the level of the heart. This means that I can, and must, redefine my life around feeling values, around being a feeling person. And when my inner hoodlum finds that I have voluntarily relocated my energy, there is no longer anything to fight about.

EPILOGUE

In the aftermath of my work on the Dream of the Four Hoodlums I was at a loss as to what to do as a ritual for my fourth step. It took me a long time to fully understand the implications of the dream. I didn't realize yet that I was going to eventually change the whole focus of my life and make feeling exchanges with people my top priority. But I knew I should do something, so I found a vacant lot, got out of my car, and walked around it a couple of times. That helped; it got me physically connected to the dream. Then I let it rest for a while.

By coincidence it happened that I traveled through Portland, Oregon, a few months later. I remembered my dream and decided that I could do a powerful ritual for reconnecting with my dream if I went back to my old neighborhood and actually walked around the places that had appeared in my dream. So it happened that I returned to the scene—of both my childhood and my fateful encounter with my feeling side.

I found Williams Avenue changed. I started at my old house and began walking over the route that I had taken in my dream. I passed the Japanese greengrocer's. The building was still there, now a beer hall. I walked on and was half-startled to find the vacant lot was still there, after all these years, overgrown with bushes and shrubbery. Irrationally, in spite of myself, I started to get scared. I was no longer in the outside world; I was in my dream.

Suddenly, as I walked slowly past the vacant lot, a young man stepped out of the bushes and approached me. Well, the time had come, I thought: I was about to be robbed, just as in the dream. He was streetwise, just like the hoodlums in the dream. He looked me over, and he sensed that I *wanted* something, that I was looking for something. Of course, he had no way of knowing that I was looking for a deeper understanding of my dream, that I was walking in my dream.

So he began to question me: Did I want marijuana? No. Then,

what about cocaine? No. Did I want a woman? No. Heroin? No. When he had exhausted his list of possibilities, he finally asked, "Well, then, what *do* you want?"

It flashed through my mind that I could tell him that I wanted to talk with the hoodlums in my dream, that I wanted to walk by the Japanese greengrocer's and the vacant lot until I connected with the parts of me that I had left there so many years before. I could have told him that I was walking in my dream and that he had walked into it and joined me. Perhaps he would have understood. But I didn't. At that point the interaction between my dream world and the physical world had become too intense for me. I walked on, got into my car, and "fled the scene."

By the time I put myself through this ritual I had touched my dream on as many levels as I could. It had become a vivid part of my life, an experience that I went back to in my mind repeatedly. Living with its symbols and the meanings that were slowly becoming more clear to me, I gradually altered my life to accord with the new conception of myself that the dream had planted in my mind.

What was that new conception? The dream forced me to realize that the most important thing in life to me is friendship and feeling-exchange with other people. I don't need to have many acquaintances, but I require good friendships that involve a deep level of communication, whether it be an exchange of ideas or the simple joy of being together.

In response to the dream I made up my mind to go to India, to visit an ancient culture where people still related to each other through the archaic ties of clan and tribe, where warmth, feeling, and human exchange are valued above logic, order, and production. The series of visits I made to India and the Orient gave me a new reference point outside the mentality that I had been reared in. I gained a concrete sense of what it is to live among people who place love and feeling and human exchange above all other values; I felt at home.

Back in the United States, the effects of my dream on me continued. I began to pull out of the standard American way of life, with the goals, the excessive work schedule, the constant feeling of pressure and deadlines, money to be made and people to be impressed. It was a slow process. But now, years later, I can say that the days of my life contrast greatly with those of the life I was leading when I dreamed of the four hoodlums. There is time for relaxation, for visiting friends, for planting in the yard, for listening to music, for Active Imagination. The succession of practical changes that made this possible began with this dream and the new attitudes that began to evolve inside me, the new conception of who I really am that began to develop in response to its symbols.

* * *

It is my hope that from the steps and the practical examples that we have explored together you will find it easier to get started on your own dream work and find the wisdom that awaits you in your own dreams. Remember that the unconscious continually expresses itself and voluntarily generates all the associations and references that you will need in order to understand your own dreams. All that is required, essentially, is your work: your willingness to begin and to follow the steps.

You may want to go beyond the bounds of this book and read more about the nature of dreams and of certain symbols or more about the ideas of Jung. You will find several books listed in the Bibliography that will help you. But basically, you will find, all that stands between you and understanding your dream is the act of writing down that first dream image, then writing down the first association that leaps into your mind.

From that first act—the crucial movement of the hand and the mind—begins all the magical and amazing unfolding of the inner mysteries that your unconscious stands ready to accomplish.

III. ACTIVE IMAGINATION

Defining and Approaching Active Imagination

In the pages ahead we will be exploring the art of Active Imagination and learning four steps for working with it. Before we begin, there is a fundamental precaution that everyone must take: *Before starting Active Imagination be sure that there is someone available for you to go to or call in case you become overwhelmed by the imagination and can't cut it off.*

For most people this is not a problem. In fact, for most people the difficulty is in getting the Active Imagination started. But some few people are subject to being so totally possessed by the flow of images, once they start a particularly powerful segment of Active Imagination, that they can't pull out of it. Their minds get lost in the realm of fantasy and can't find the way back to the here-and-now of the ordinary world. Therefore I advise people to start Active Imagination only after they have available to them either an analyst or a layperson who is familiar with the art and could talk them back down to earth if required.

Once in a while one will do Active Imagination in the morning, go to work or start the daily schedule, and then find the imagination returning, taking over the conscious mind, trying to continue the story or dialogue where it left off earlier in the day. When this happens, it may be difficult to keep one's mind on the task at hand. In this case, it is best to call one's therapist or friend and get some help in pulling out of the involuntarily recurring Active Imagination.

In the rare cases of people who get easily lost in the fantasy realm and can't find their way back, it is better that they not do Active Imagination but find cooler ways of relating to their inner world.

In you have any doubts about this, it would be advisable to consult with a Jungian analyst before undertaking this technique.

This is not meant to discourage you from doing inner work, but the unconscious is powerful: If we are going to approach it, respect and care are in order. With this attitude, we can derive the benefits of inner work while still protecting ourselves from the sometimes overwhelming power of the unconscious.

DISTINGUISHING ACTIVE IMAGINATION FROM PASSIVE FANTASY

Active Imagination is a special use of the power of imagination that Jung developed early in this century. Although many people have used it and its tremendous value is well proven, it is not widely known outside Jungian circles. Of those who have heard of it, many feel they do not understand it well enough to put it into practice.

In this section we will explore the basic concepts of Active Imagination, look at some examples, and learn a step-by-step approach that you can follow in doing your own Active Imagination.

Essentially, Active Imagination is a dialogue that you enter into with the different parts of yourself that live in the unconscious. In some ways it is similar to dreaming, except that you are fully awake and conscious during the experience. This, in fact, is what gives this technique its distinctive quality. Instead of going into a dream, you go into your imagination while you are awake. You allow the images to rise up out of the unconscious, and they come to you on the level of imagination just as they would come to you in dream if you were asleep.

In your imagination you begin to talk to your images and interact with them. They answer back. You are startled to find out that they express radically different viewpoints from those of your conscious mind. They tell you things you never consciously knew and express thoughts that you never consciously thought.

Most people do a fair amount of talking in their Active Imagination, exchanging points of view with the inner figures, trying to work out a middle ground between opposing views, even asking for advice from some very wise ones who live in the unconscious. But not all dialogue is verbal or spoken.

Probably the earliest recorded experience of Active Imagination in its modern form was a visionary experience of Jung in which no words were spoken, yet there was a profound interaction between his conscious mind and the images that appeared to him from the unconscious. This was one of the experiences that demonstrated to Jung that he could go into his fantasy or vision, participate consciously in it, and make it into an active exchange between the conscious and unconscious energy systems.

> I was sitting at my desk once more, thinking over my fears. Then I let myself drop. Suddenly it was as though the ground literally gave way beneath my feet, and I plunged down into dark depths. I could not fend off a feeling of panic. But then, abruptly, at not too great a depth, I landed on my feet in a soft, sticky mass. I felt great relief, although I was apparently in complete darkness. After a while my eyes grew accustomed to the gloom, which was rather like a deep twilight. Before me was the entrance to a dark cave, in which stood a dwarf with a leathery skin, as if he were mummified. I squeezed past him through the narrow entrance and waded knee-deep through icy water to the other end of the cave where, on a projecting rock, I saw a glowing red crystal. I grasped the stone, lifted it, and discovered a hollow underneath. At first I could make out nothing, but then I saw that there was running water. In it a corpse floated by, a youth with blond hair and a wound in the head. He was followed by a gigantic black scarab and then by a red, newborn sun, rising up out of the depths of the water . . . (Jung, *MDR*, p. 179)

Through Active Imagination it becomes more and more clear that the images that appear in imagination are in fact *symbols*, representing deep interior parts of ourselves. Like dream images, they symbolize the contents of our unconscious. Because these interior beings have "minds of their own," they say and do things that are new to us—startling, often enlightening, sometimes offensive to our egos.

Although Jung held dreams in high regard, he considered Active Imagination to be an even more effective path to the unconscious. The difference is this: When you dream, you receive signals from the unconscious, but the conscious mind does not participate. When you wake up, the conscious mind can remember the dream and think about its meaning, but during the dream itself, the conscious mind cannot actively participate. In Active Imagination, by contrast, the conscious mind is awake. It participates consciously in the events.

In dreams, the events happen completely at the unconscious level. In Active Imagination, the events take place on the *imaginative* level, which is neither conscious nor unconscious but a meeting place, a common ground where both meet on equal terms and together create a life experience that combines the elements of both. The two levels of consciousness flow into each other in the field of imagination like two rivers that merge to form one powerful stream. They complement each other; they begin to work together; and, as a result, your totality begins to form itself into a unity. The dialogue of conscious mind with unconscious gives rise to the transcendent function, the self, that stands as the synthesis of the two.

It is a curious fact that dreaming decreases dramatically when one does Active Imagination. If you take this art seriously as a way of meditation, you actually assimilate the material of the unconscious before it needs to come up in dream form. The issues that would have been presented in dreams are confronted and worked out through Active Imagination.

Because of this relationship between dreams and Active Imagination, Jung used to prescribe Active Imagination for people who were dreaming too much, who were overwhelmed by too many dreams every night and couldn't keep up with them by dream work. When you begin to do Active Imagination regularly, you will find that your dreams decrease in number, will become more focused and concentrated and less repetitious. As you deal with the issues in Active Imagination, your dreams have less need to repeat themselves.

The essence of Active Imagination is your *conscious participation* in the imaginative experience. This kind of imagination is *active* because the ego actually goes into the inner world, walks and talks, confronts and argues, makes friends with or fights with the persons it finds there. You consciously take part in the drama in your imagination. You engage the other actors in conversation, exchange viewpoints, go through adventures together, and eventually learn something from each other.

This quality makes Active Imagination different from ordinary, *passive* fantasy. Passive fantasy is daydreaming: It is sitting and merely watching the stream of fantasy that goes on in the back of your mind as though you were at a movie. In passive fantasy you do not consciously participate; you do not reflect on what is happening; and you do not take an independent, ethical position regarding what is going on.

Passive fantasy also presents images from the unconscious. But since we can't consciously enter into it, it is mostly a waste of time and energy. The issues or problems that come up in the fantasy don't get resolved. Most such fantasies just repeat themselves over and over again on the edges of our minds until they exhaust themselves or exhaust us. There is no evolution, because the ego never confronts the fantasy situation or enters into it as a conscious, independent force.

A good example of this is the phenomenon of *worry*. Worry is one form of passive fantasy. Most of us have subjects that we worry about day in and day out. A fantasy runs through our minds in which we triumph and everything works out well. Then the counterfantasy, the worry fantasy, arises in which we are defeated and humiliated. So long as we sit passively and let the worry fantasies possess us, there is never a resolution, but in Active Imagination it is possible to go to the worry, actively confront it, enter into dialogue with it, find out who or what is in conflict within us, and do something about it.

You will notice in all the examples of Active Imagination we look at that the story is always related in the first person: The "I" is always there. "I" go to a certain place. "I" see the image. "I" interact with it. The "I" has to be there, interacting with the other characters, or else the ego would not be participating.

It is not *active* unless you are participating in the drama with your feelings and emotions. "I" have a feeling reaction: I am happy with what happens, interested, sad, or angry. The "I" must enter into the imaginative act as intensely as it would if it were an external, physical experience. Although it is a symbolic experience, it is still a real experience involving real feelings.

By your active participation you convert what would have been an unconscious, passive fantasy into a highly conscious, powerful act of the imagination. When Active Imagination is done correctly, it pulls the different parts of you together that have been fragmented or in conflict; it wakens you powerfully to the voices inside you; and it brings about peace and cooperation between the warring ego and unconscious.

The main purpose of this art is to provide communication between the ego and the parts of the unconscious that we are usually cut off from. When you do Active Imagination, things *change* in the psyche. The relationship between the ego and the unconscious is altered. If there is a neurotic imbalance between the attitudes of ego and the values of the unconscious, the gap can be narrowed, the complementary opposites can be brought together. It sets one off on a path toward wholeness, toward an awareness of one's larger totality, simply because one has learned to enter into communication with the inner self.

ACTIVE IMAGINATION EXAMPLE: TALKING WITH THE INNER ARTIST

In order to make our discussion more concrete from the beginning, I will give you an example now of a session of Active Imagination recorded by a woman. This will be the first in a series of examples that we will look at in the next few chapters. These examples should give you a better idea of what ordinary people actually do, in practice, when they sit down to experience Active Imagination: how they approach it, how they write it out, and the different purposes that Active Imagination can serve in your own inner work.

One point should come clear from these examples: You should not try to "dress up" your imagination and make it sound proper, grammatical, or "refined." The object is to experience and record whatever flows out of your unconscious honestly in its raw, spontaneous form. You are not doing creative writing for other people's eyes. This is a private matter between you and your own unconscious, between you and God, so let it be as rough, crude, incoherent, embarrassing, beautiful, or unregenerate as it may be when it comes spontaneously out of your unconscious. The results will be more honest—and more real.

This particular sample of Active Imagination comes from a woman who found herself lying awake one night, unable to sleep because she had become obsessed during the repainting of her house. She had worked herself into a state of exhaustion, choosing colors, buying paint, doing the work. But she found herself unable to sleep because color combinations and different ways to combine colors, fabrics, and furniture passed through her mind half the night in a fantasy she could not turn off.

Since she had used Active Imagination before, she thought of going into her imagination to find an image that would represent the obsession. She wanted to find the one within her who was obsessed and dialogue with that part of herself.

This is an example of one of the finest uses of Active Imagination: *to personify an unseen content of the unconscious* and bring it to the surface, in image form, so that you can dialogue with it and deal with it.

We often have something vague and invisible in the unconscious that bothers us. We can feel the conflict just below the surface, but we can't see what is going on. We can't associate it with anything specific or concrete. We feel the effect, but otherwise it is so vague and formless that we can't "get a handle on it." Sometimes it is an inexplicable, free-floating anger. We can't say why we are angry, or at what—we just feel it. Moods, worries, depressions, inflations, and obsessions all come within this category.

When this happens, you can go to the unconscious in your imagination and ask the unseen content to personify itself. You can start your Active Imagination by asking: "Where is the obsession? Who is obsessed? Where does this feeling come from? Who is the one inside me who feels this way? What is its image? What does he or she look like?"

If you do this, an image eventually comes into your mind. The image may personify the obsession itself, or it may represent the part of you that is generating the effect—the one who is obsessed, depressed, moody, or angry.

Here is this woman's experience as it flowed out of her in the middle of the night. She wrote some explanatory notes afterwards, which are enclosed in parentheses; otherwise, it is what she wrote into her notebook that night as it came out of her imagination:

(While repainting the interior of our house, an exuberance for color and design, texture and balance, arose. As the plans progressed, however, this "interest" took over my mind completely. I was unable to sleep, kept awake by an endless fantasy of palettes of colors and arrays of design. What had begun as an interesting project became an obsession.

The process had taken on a life of its own; it was harnessing all my resources; it functioned completely outside my conscious control. Although great energy was released, I was getting depleted. I was impatient and irritable toward my husband, who couldn't understand my great zeal.

It wasn't enough to discipline myself, to label this great energy in me as "negative animus" or an attachment. Although I felt this obsession as a "negative" force, I sensed that it was not so much negative as out of proportion. There was a new wellspring of vitality that had not been tapped. To control it by behavioral means would only repress this new resource back into the shadow. I would lose access to it. So I asked, "What is it that has suddenly taken hold of me?" In the middle of the night I entered into a dialogue with that "energy" inside me to find out who it was and what it wanted.)

My Active Imagination

(As I wrote it down in my notebook, E represents "ego," my conscious mind speaking. JA represents the voice that was revealed after awhile to be a Japanese artist. I could not see the figure who was speaking at first.)

E: What is happening here? I've been taken over by an unknown force. I can't sleep for the barrage of hues before my eyes. What are you doing? What do you want? Who are you?

(Voice): (Sounds like a feminine voice in my imagination.) The colors are so lovely. See the interplay. See how they evoke different aspects of nature. These, in particular, go so well with the wood tones of the bookshelves—

E: Excuse me. Yes, it is indeed lovely, but I am very weary and I have other considerations in life to worry about. I have other things to balance with this effort. You have taken over.

(At this point I began to realize that the feminine voice inside me was not so much obsessed as thrilled at the colors.)

(Voice): I have a clear idea of what wants to be created here. I am trying to find the right tools. We must find the right fabric and paint and design to make it happen, to make it physical.

E: That is fine. But must you do it all night???

JA: Oh. Yes. I see what you mean.

(The figure grows clearer to me. This is a Japanese figure. At first it looked like a masculine figure, but now I see that it is neither masculine nor feminine, but androgynous. I feel that this is an artist, dressed in orange Zen Buddhist robes. The being stays silent, as though wounded. I am suddenly "tracking" on this being's personality, and I "know" that it has sensitivity, a vision derived from a meticulous appreciation of physical nature. I feel that I don't want to lose this being. I feel my irritation and frustration evaporating. I am getting very interested in this creature.)

E: Please don't retreat. I am not angry. We can come to an agreement so that we both can thrive. Why are you pushing me so hard?

JA: I am afraid.

E: Afraid of what?

JA: I am afraid that I will be locked up again.

E: Locked up?

JA: There are rarely any opportunities for me to express myself. It seems I must work very fast and intensely while the door is open to me. Soon it will be over, and I will be locked up again.

E: I begin to see what you mean. In my life there have been very few outlets provided for you, so few that I hardly knew you existed. The culture I live in doesn't provide any place for you. And I have not stood separately from my culture in this matter to provide for you.

JA: That is true. I feel that I've been starving. This may be my only opportunity.

E: It doesn't have to be. If I provided other vehicles for you, other ways to express yourself, would you feel less desperate? Could you decrease your intensity?

JA: Yes . . .

(There is a long pause. Then the being speaks very gently.)

Do you—are you aware of what that implies?

E: (I feel apprehensive. I am about to commit myself to something that perhaps I can't back out of.)

I think so. I know it hasn't been easy for me to give permission to purely creative efforts in the physical and sensation world. I have always let practicality get in the way. I always feel the pressure of my work, my responsibilities.

JA: I have tried to express myself through you, but for the most part those "practical" matters always win out. The pure joy of creating, living in the physical side of life, is whole unto itself—without expectation of outcome or so-called practical benefits.

E: This is true. And, given my conditioning, my dominant attitudes, I know you had to make me uncomfortable to get my attention. I see that I will have to stand independent of the values of productivity that surround me and dominate me. I must deal with the negative masculine production mentality that carries these ideas and crowds out everything else. He uses my fear of failure, my performance anxieties. And I must confront my *desire* to produce, to be a success in my work, that gets out of hand. I must sort through the values connected with art, artistic expression in the physical world, and I must make a place for you. More directly, I have to provide some immediate vehicles for you. What do you suggest?

JA: Something like ceramics, watercolors. Plant flowers. Arrange flowers. Or you can do something less formal. I just want us to work and play with form and color and aspects of the physical world.

E: Fine. I will need your help also. I need your awareness of the value of the sensation world to strengthen me against the prejudice that has ruled me.

JA: You only need to still yourself and call to me, and I will respond. I will come back to you.

There is an interesting footnote to this session of Active Imagination: the feeling reaction and the meanings that this woman drew from her experience:

I resisted the language in which this Active Imagination was expressed. All these clichés about "creativity" and getting "into" ceramics and "into" watercolors seemed trite. But I also understood that, no matter how the language came out, and no matter whether I felt I was being faddish or silly, the physical and sensation side of me had to be nourished. I had to deal with that part of me on its own terms and do what it needed of me, within reason.

The figure of the Japanese artist made me confront the degree to which my culture discourages an awareness of beauty. This culture is interested only in productivity and empiricism. It assigns no value to *being*, as opposed to *doing*. It gives no value to beauty that exists in its own right without utilitarian production. The dialogue with this newly discovered ally led to a long investigation of the cultural prejudices I had absorbed by virtue of being born here. It helped me to sort out my individual nature from the collective. In other words, it was part of my individuation process.

In the aftermath of this Active Imagination, this woman found a new world opening up to her. She talked to this inner Japanese artist figure regularly. She started a class in ceramics. She spends a certain amount of time every week working in her garden or at the ceramics workshop and in other physical or artistic activities that bring her a sense of beauty and put her in contact with earth-connected, feminine values.

As you know from her dialogue, she had been so tied up with mental work—thinking, analyzing, productivity—that there was no room in her life for the physical side of life, the realm of physical beauty, the sense of being connected through the physical body to the earth, the plants, the colors and textures that intoxicate her inner Zen monk.

So she has derived a deep satisfaction from all this, a knowledge that she is nourishing a part of herself that was starving before. And her sense of who she is has been amplified accordingly. There is more to her than she had realized.

Any quality within you can be personified in this way and persuaded to clothe itself in an image so that you can interact with it. If you feel an inflation, you can go to your imagination and ask that inflation to personify itself through an image. If you vaguely feel a mood controlling you, you can do the same. It is the image that gives one a starting point. You can then enter into dialogue; you can interact; and you can move toward some kind of understanding.

In this example you find all the basic elements necessary for good Active Imagination. Please notice that the whole experience began in a kind of passive fantasy. As this woman lay in bed, colors and images of infinite possibilities floated before her eyes. At that point she was merely a spectator, possessed by the fantasy.

She converted this fantasy into Active Imagination precisely at the point where she stood outside the fantasy as a conscious ego-mind, as an independent force in her own right, and then began to take an active role. She began to ask some questions and expect some answers. She looked for the one who was behind all this, who was generating this stream of fantasy. As a result, the image was constellated and the conversation could begin.

Another indication that this is real Active Imagination is that she was involved with her *feelings* in what was going on. She was upset with the situation, but she was also concerned and moved when she found that there was a strong part of her inner self that had been ignored and repressed. She valued that part of herself; she appreciated it; she had feelings toward it. This is shown not only by what she said but by her *doing something* afterwards to honor that part of herself.

Another important factor was her willingness to listen to the person from the unconscious. She did not try to dominate or override the inner voice. She was willing to let it have its say and to learn from it.

There are many concepts relating to Active Imagination that we will explore in the chapters ahead. But already in this example you have the basic principles you will need in order to do genuine Active Imagination. If you hold them firmly in mind, you are already launched on the path toward understanding and using this high art.

WHEN YOU THINK YOU'RE MAKING UP SOMETHING

A new patient came to do analysis with me. He was an intelligent man—but I could sense that he was also a rogue. You could feel it when he walked in for his first session; there was a certain look in his eye.

For the first few sessions nothing happened. He could remember no dreams, and there was no significant discussion. I wondered why he was interested in analysis at all. So I taught him about Active Imagination, thinking that this would be the way to unlock his unconscious and find out what was going on inside him.

At first nothing happened. No Active Imagination. I explained the four steps and said: "Go do something in your imagination—anything! Just record it in your journal. We will start from there."

The next week he returned, and he had that gleam in his eye again. I knew he was up to something. He put down a couple of pages of Active Imagination. It was hair-raising material. It was pure melodrama, a combination of *The Perils of Pauline* and two generations of *Peyton Place* all rolled into one.

After that, week after week, he brought his pages of Active Imagination. The events got more intense, more desperate. It was huge battles of darkness against light, villains and victims, persecuted heroines, scandalous intrigues, and betrayals. The poor girl was jumping from ice floe to ice floe with babe in arms, crossing the river with the villain in hot pursuit.

Week after week this went on, and I said very little. It was registering, but I watched to see where all this inner drama was leading, what was going to distill out of it.

One day he came in and dramatically threw down the last installment of the Active Imagination. There I read a terrible, but also marvelous, denouement of the plot that had been developing all this time. When I finished reading he said: "There, you bloody idiot! I've been pulling your leg the whole time. I've been making the whole thing up just to make a fool out of you. There wasn't a word of truth in it!"

I said nothing, but I thought: "Well, not the first time someone has made a fool of me." Then I just sat and waited. I looked at him, and I'll never forget the change that came over his face. The triumphant expression changed slowly to one of horror. Tears came to his eyes. He said: "Damn you, damn you, damn you! You tricked me. It was all true, and I didn't know it." Then he just fell apart.

You see, even when he was trying to conjure up his "fake" story in order to fool me and ridicule the whole process, that "fake" story had to come out of his own insides, his own psychological "guts," as it were. While he thought he was inventing something, he was spilling out the secret contents of his interior being.

That horrible villain in the story was none other than the rogue who gave him the sly gleam in his eye, who controlled him so much from hidden places—the same rogue who believed that the whole point of analysis was to make an ass out of the analyst. The persecuted heroines were none other than his own inner feminine side: His inner life and feeling life were consigned to the ice floes. All the intrigues, innocent victims, tragedies, and adventures were an involuntary reflection of the horrible conflicts that raged within his own soul.

He had tried to fake it. But accidentally, in the process he did his Active Imagination. He experienced the symbols from the unconscious. Finally, his Active Imagination brought him face-to-face with his inner self. He was never quite the same again.

Whenever I start a patient on Active Imagination, I get a series of questions: "How do I know that I'm not just making all this stuff up?" "How can I talk with someone who is only a figment of my imagination?" From my experience I am convinced that it is nearly impossible to produce anything in the imagination that is not an authentic representation of something in the unconscious. The whole function of the imagination is to draw up the material from the unconscious, clothe it in images, and transmit it to the conscious mind. Whatever comes up in the imagination must have been living somewhere in the fabric of the unconscious before it was given an image-form by the imagination.

Even if a person is frivolous and deliberately tries to fabricate something, to conjure up something silly and stupid, to imagine a pure fiction, the material that comes up through the imagination still represents some hidden part of that individual. It can't be made up from thin air. It has to come from somewhere inside the person who is producing the images.

The real question is not the authenticity of the images, but rather, *What do I do with them?* It is easy to misunderstand them and misuse them. But most people never get to the real question of what to do with the revelation from the unconscious because they are so stuck in doubting its authenticity.

Once, after a lecture, a man asked me: "But, how do I know I am not just talking with my superego?" Sometimes you *are* talking with your superego, or that part of the psyche that can be called the superego. It quotes the law and tells you to conform to the ideas of right and wrong that your parents handed you, to the conventional ideas of your culture. Perhaps you, as an evolving ego consciousness, are answering back, saying that you have to question those things and think for yourself. The point is that you are talking with a part of *yourself*—and that is exactly the object of all this.

Another patient said: "But I just feel as though I'm talking to myself." My reply was: "Fine. You are talking to your various *selves*. That is the whole point."

If you feel that you are talking to yourself, excellent! If you feel you are "making it up," as my sly patient did, that is fine. Whatever you make up will come from your unconscious; it will be one of your interior personalities speaking. All that is required, ultimately, is that you write down what you have to say, write down what the interior persons have to say, and write down what you do together. When you begin to see your imagination for what it really is, you will realize that it reflects the inner world of your unconscious as faithfully as a highly polished mirror.

Active Imagination as
Mythic Journey

The Active Imagination in the following example is quite different from what we have seen so far. Often when people begin a
series of Active Imaginations, what comes out has little to do with
any immediate issue in their personal lives. As in this example,
their experience seems more like a mythical adventure, a journey
into the archetypal realm. It takes them off to the court of King
Arthur, or to the glades of ancient Greece when the gods were
walking in plain view.

Unless we understood that such adventures are symbolic experiences of some great theme being played out in our unconscious,
we would jump to the wrong conclusions. We would think this was
merely entertainment, some fictional story that the writer has
tossed off merely for enjoyment. As you will see, the following example sounds like the beginning of a great myth—a journey into
a land where evil is afoot, a heroic quest to help an innocent
queen, a task of healing the sick and wounded.

But the story is not fictional in the deepest sense, for every detail of it is absolutely true for the one who is passing through it in
imagination. Sometimes great works of fiction do begin as Active
Imagination. But at the moment that the story came out of the
author's mind, it was not fiction; it was a true representation of a
dynamic deep in the unconscious, expressing itself symbolically
through the imagination.

If you find yourself meeting an inner guide and being led off on a
mythical adventure, it will help if you understand that this is a legitimate and excellent way to live out parts of yourself that can't be
lived fully in your immediate, daily, physical life. Such mythical
journeys also may be rites of passage: As we grow, as we move from
one level of maturity to the next, there is always some great archetypal theme that must be confronted, some conflict that must be
resolved at deep levels where we are scarcely aware of them.

Each of us has all the great archetypal themes hidden inside. We all have the seeds of the heroic quest within us; we must live it out sometime, on some level. Each of us has the journey and labors of Psyche, the encounter with Eros and Aphrodite, built somewhere into our inner structure. One can't avoid these archetypal leitmotivs; one must express and experience them.

Active Imagination is one of the best and most legitimate levels on which to live these experiences. A few people are able to go off to the jungles of the Amazon, take part in a revolution, become war correspondents, or in some way live out the heroic quest on an external level. Most of us, however, have relationships, commitments, families, and all the normal, practical limits that prevent us from extroverting this great primordial energy system within us. So what are we to do?

The man in this example is a professional with an office and a busy daily schedule. He has a family and other people who depend on him. He wouldn't, and shouldn't, break all this up and go charging off to feudal lands looking for an innocent queen to defend. But within his soul he also has the life of a man of the Renaissance, a hero and a healer. He has the archetypal battle of light and darkness, of masculine power drive and the feminine soul, of external practicality and the inner, mystical vision. These great themes live in his unconscious, but they are greater than anything that is going on in his local, personal life. They express themselves in the magnitude of the mythical adventure that pours out of his imagination.

This example represents only one session out of a long series of Active Imaginations that this man has done on this theme. Every day, or as often as he has time, he goes back to his Active Imagination, takes up where he left off, and continues the saga that is spinning itself out within him. This is often the case with Active Imagination. You will get an adventure going, or a profound conversation started with an inner character, and you will find yourself returning to the same place over and over to continue where you left off. In this way the series may continue for days, weeks, or even months.

Before we start, there are a few things that you should note: First, please observe this man's way of *starting* the Active Imagination. He goes to a bridge that is in a place like Renaissance Europe, and there he finds the "man with the feathered cap, the Renaissance man who is teacher and guide." By going to an established place in your imagination and meeting up with such a guide (whom we often call *psychopomps* because they guide us through the psyche), you can get your Active Imagination started directly and quickly each time.

Second, please notice that this man has adopted a special ritual way of getting himself back and forth between the inner world of dreaming/imagination and the external world of human life. When he is ready to go to the inner world in Active Imagination, he puts on a blue monk's cowl in his imagination. This symbolizes for him his intention to enter into his inner world and into religious experience. When he is ready to leave the world of imagination and return to the daily human world, he gets up from his desk and puts on a plaid flannel shirt that his wife gave him. By putting on that shirt he reaffirms his other commitment, to his wife, to his family, to the earthbound world of daily, physical human life.

Now, here is his session of Active Imagination, as he copied it out of his notebook:

> (Greetings from the man with the feathered cap, the Renaissance man, who is teacher and guide. He greets me at the bridge. He has his staff. I have brought my lantern and a backpack.)

MAN: Greetings! I bring you good tidings. The weather is good for our journey tonight. We must begin right away, however, for things can change quickly in this world. Let us begin while we have the energy.

I: I am willing to begin this journey. I am willing to stick it through to its end. I begin in good faith that my actions will be sufficient to please the fates and they will be kind to me.

MAN: Let us begin, then, and remember: Even the smallest effort is of value . . . what matters is that we persevere. I am here to help you on this journey. Let us take the first steps together and set on our way. Remember one thing—worldly matters do not matter here.

I: I live in the physical world; however, I am only a visitor here, and I do have outer responsibilities that may call me away. All I can do is say so, then I must go. The ritual will be that I will put on my plaid flannel shirt my wife has given me and then I will leave. I will put on my blue monk's robe to enter into your world. This will be the ritual. I will come here as often as I can without injuring my outer relationships and responsibilities.

MAN: Agreed. This is a good ritual, and it does not offend me or the lady that I serve, who sent me to fetch you.

I: Why has she sent you to fetch me?

MAN: She needs your help, your assistance. There is trouble in her land. This is a troubled time; evil is afoot. She needs your assistance—as much as you can give her.

I: I will do the best I can.

MAN: She appreciates this . . . and loves you for it. I have been faithful to her for many years.

I: How did you come to know her?

MAN: Through the service of my king who died recently. He was single when I first came to his service twenty-five years ago. He married the Queen a year later: He had invited a neighboring lord to hunt on his land in thanks for some small favor the lord had paid him. When the lord came, he brought his daughter, fifteen years younger than the king. He fell in love with her and courted her during their stay for two weeks. They married, and in my loyal service I have grown close to the Queen. The King's health had failed the past two years before he died, and of course his enemies have tried to profit by this fact. His army and lords have been faithful and have held strong, but there is some subtle evil afoot and the Queen senses it.

I: Why did she ask for my help?

MAN: Because a new star appeared in our eastern sky at night that is four-pointed, and we have never seen such a star before. The Queen keeps a wise old man to counsel her on such matters. He advised our waiting on that spot on the horizon where the star first appeared. It happens that that spot is this bridge where you and I first met. We called you, and you appeared. We called you in your dreams.

(At this moment I have to pause in our long walk. I put on my plaid flannel shirt to attend to business in the outer world.)

(Later, I return. I put on my blue robe to enter the inner world again and find the man in the feathered hat.)

I: I am back.

MAN: Let us begin our journey again. So this is the story in brief of her whom I have come to know and serve—the Queen—and of the evil that is about since my king's death.

I: What kind of evil is it?

MAN: Abusive evil! Evil that must be stopped. A small village was pillaged, the men murdered, put to the sword, male children killed, women raped and killed, little girls the same, babies left to die. In total, thirty people murdered most cruelly. And the real mischief is that the murderers were dressed as king's men, and the rumor that goes through the villages is that the Queen is a witch who wishes to dominate them and steal their possessions. But I know the Queen. She is a good woman, and this is against her nature. She has a young daughter of her own, eighteen years old. She is a tender woman. The Queen has sent out a search party for the villains, but no luck finding them as of yet.

I: Is that all?

MAN: No! There is an unlucky sickness about. Two children have died, and no one has seen such a thing, a sweet smell on their mouths, but death. And there is a young girl in this village just ahead who is at death's door, it seems. Swollen foot and fever . . . wasting away.

       (We come to the outskirts of a village. There is a thatched hut and a fire burning inside. The man knocks and we enter. The mother is distraught and tired—tears in her eyes. The father is the same—toughened, weathered people whose greatest possession is this young daughter of theirs, perhaps eight years old, blond hair and features that would be beautiful if she were not so sick. She looks very pale, dark hued under her eyes, and her breath is labored. She is feverish and racked with chills. She has been ill for three days, and her parents do not know the cause. Her left foot is swollen. The man introduces me as a healer who has come to offer help. Their eyes look pleading.

(We undress the little girl. I examine her and find all to be normal except for a small point of entry in the base of her left foot. There is pus. I tell them to hold her down. The mother faints at the sight of my knife, but the father and my guide hold the girl down while I lance the foot. A cup of pus pours forth. I find imbedded in the flesh an arrowhead made of flint and covered with a black resinous substance. I keep this and wrap it up carefully.

I give the girl a cool bath. I tell the family to boil water so we can clean the wound. We clean the wound. I then instruct them on cleansing bandages, boiling them, drying them in the sun, soaking her foot, and giving her broth made from meat. I tell them I must leave and go back to my world, but I will return later. I tell them she will live. I put on my plaid flannel shirt and leave the inner world.)

This excerpt presents us with a completely different purpose for which Active Imagination can be used, and a different style. The purpose, in this example, is not to work out some immediate problem or conflict at the personal level. It is, rather, to make a place in one's life where the great archetypal themes can live themselves out.

This kind of Active Imagination connects us to the timeless cosmic dance of the archetypes that goes on eternally at the level of the unconscious. It is a way of discovering how those universal energy systems flow through us as individuals, how they particularize themselves and express themselves in a unique and special way within the container of our individual personalities. They seem distant and superpersonal; they seem to have nothing to do with our immediate personal lives. Yet they are the building blocks of our personalities and our life experiences. They are the elements that make us up.

By going to Active Imagination, letting the archetypal themes take on symbolic form, and participating in the drama, we transform the situation. The archetypal forces no longer play themselves out offstage, out of sight in the collective unconscious, but come up to the conscious level through imagination. We, in our ego forms, actually enter into the play of the archetypes and actually influence the outcome of the drama. In the deepest sense, this symbolic interaction with the archetypes puts us in the remarkable position of playing a role in the working out of fate.

We cannot readily say where it is in this man's structure that the innocent queen is under attack by the forces of masculine power drive. We can't say where the sick little girl is who has been pierced by a poisoned arrow. It is not even particularly helpful to analyze these things, for the main point in Active Imagination is that one *experience* it. Unlike dream work, where it is so important to analyze and draw meanings from the symbols, it can be counterproductive in Active Imagination if you distract yourself by thinking too much about what the symbols may mean in psychological terms. The magic of Active Imagination comes about through the experience itself. Once the series of Active Imaginations has reached its resolution, it is permissible to draw meanings from it and to try to understand what the symbols add up to. But don't let analytical thinking get in the way of the experience while it is happening.

In all of *us* the same archetypal queen and the same sick little girl struggle to survive, caught in a momentous battle of power that is waged ceaselessly, out of sight and out of time, in a borderland that lies along the frontier between personal psyche and collective unconscious.

So long as we leave that battle out there, in a realm of twilight at the edges of the universe, we can take no part in bringing this dynamic to a resolution. But by giving this cosmic clash—of light and dark, feminine and masculine, queen and villain—a symbolic form, by bringing it up to the surface, we make it possible for the conscious ego to be aware of this huge play of forces. It can participate in the cosmic drama, play its part and have its say, and actually influence the long-range outcome. It becomes possible to consciously and voluntarily enter into the life of the archetypes that surround us, rather than sit helpless and mute, determined by powers that we can neither see nor understand.

At first this may seem rather esoteric, or unrelated to "real life." But you may be sure that this man's act of participation in the great archetypal epic, his healing of the sick child, his going with aid to the innocent queen, will make a difference in his life. Something specific and real is healed, deep inside, in response to a symbolic act of this quality.

It will profoundly alter the long-range course of his life, the contours of his character. He will be acting eventually from a different center if he keeps up this Active Imagination, creating a different balance among the powers that make him up and invest him with energy. His attitude will alter; his choices will be changed—he will be different.

The Four-Step Approach to Active Imagination

In the next few chapters I will present a four-step approach to Active Imagination that you can use to get yourself started. In this chapter we will talk about the approach overall and also about the things you need to do to set the stage for Active Imagination. For example, you need to know where you will work; you need to establish some privacy; and you need to decide how you are going to record your Active Imagination.

Here are the four steps:

1. Invite the unconscious
2. Dialogue and experience
3. Add the ethical element of values.
4. Make it concrete with physical ritual

Dr. Maria Louise Von Franz has shown that Active Imagination naturally falls into four basic stages.* Different people will experience these stages in slightly different ways. I have tried, with these four practical steps, to formulate an orderly approach that will enable most people to find their way through the stages of Active Imagination without getting paralyzed or intimidated.

Just as with dream work, it helps greatly to have a set procedure, a series of steps you can follow in an orderly way, that will get you past the obstacles, confusion, and indecision that sometimes prevent people from getting started or following through.

CHOOSING A PHYSICAL MODE FOR RECORDING YOUR IMAGINATION

Before we launch into the four steps, it is vital that you get the physical details of your method worked out. You need to set the

---

* The four stages enumerated by Dr. Von Franz are: (1) empty the ego-mind; (2) let the unconscious flow into the vacuum; (3) add the ethical element; (4) integrate the imagination back into daily life. (Unpublished lecture, Panarian Conference, Los Angeles, 1979.)

physical stage and decide how you are going to record your Active Imagination.

These details are more important than you might think. Many people give up on Active Imagination before they get started because they can't find a convenient way to record the imagination as it flows out.

We have already talked about the importance of writing your inner work. This is even more true of Active Imagination. Your inner dialogue should be written or typed. This is your major protection against turning it into just another passive fantasy. The writing helps you to focus on what you are doing, and not wander off into random daydreams. It enables you to record what is said and done so that you will remember and digest the experience afterwards.

Writing is not the only mode of recording your Active Imagination. Later I will mention some other approaches. But for most people writing is the easiest, most effective way.

HOW TO WRITE

The two samples of Active Imagination I have given so far show a typical format for writing down the imagination. In the first sample, the woman used her notebook and wrote everything out by hand. She indicated who was speaking by an abbreviation in the margin: *E* stands for ego (meaning herself) and JA for the Japanese artist with whom she dialogued.

I use the typewriter to record my own imagination. If you are proficient with the typewriter, it is very helpful. You can record your imagination rapidly, and you don't tire as quickly as you do if you write by hand. Nevertheless many people prefer to write by hand, and this was the mode used by Jung. Some people feel that the use of pen and ink feels more "natural." They may even give their Active Imagination a ceremonial or archaic flavor by recording it with fine calligraphy.

My own method has worked well for many people who at first had difficulty getting started. I use the lowercase setting on the typewriter to type what I am saying, and I use the shift-lock (uppercase, all capitals) on the typewriter to record what the other person in my imagination says back to me. In this way I don't even have to indent or paragraph when there is a change of speaker. I shift on the typewriter when I change speakers, and I can move along as fast as my imagination flows.

If the man whose mythic journey was the second example of Active Imagination had used my method, his Active Imagination would have looked like this:

(Greetings from the man with the feathered cap, the Renaissance man, who is teacher and guide. He greets me at the bridge. He has his staff. I have brought my lantern and a backpack.) GREET-INGS! I BRING YOU GOOD TIDINGS. THE WEATHER IS GOOD FOR OUR JOURNEY TONIGHT. WE MUST BEGIN RIGHT AWAY, HOWEVER, FOR THINGS CAN CHANGE QUICKLY IN THIS WORLD. LET US BEGIN WHILE WE HAVE THE ENERGY. I am willing to begin this journey. I am willing to stick it through to its end. I begin in good faith that my actions will be sufficient to please the fates and they will be kind to me. LET US BEGIN, THEN, AND REMEMBER: EVEN THE SMALLEST EFFORT IS OF VALUE . . .

As you can see, the writer's words are in lowercase, and the words of the Renaissance man are in uppercase. If you use this method, you don't have to keep writing "I" or "Man" in the margin to identify who is speaking, and you don't have to worry about indenting, paragraphing, or quotation marks. When you see the lowercase you know it is you speaking, and when you see the uppercase it is the other person talking. In this way you can just pour the dialogue and events onto the page as quickly as they happen, and keep moving.

There is no need to stop and make corrections: No one other than you will be reading it.

If this format suits you, use it. If not, try the approach that was used in the earlier examples—or work a method out for yourself. The important thing is to have a simple, easy way to record what happens and what is said during the session of Active Imagina-tion. If you have to struggle with quotation marks, sentence struc-ture, punctuation, and spelling, you are already defeated before you start: It will feel too cumbersome and you won't continue. Adopt a method that is direct, simple, and works for you.

OTHER WAYS OF REGISTERING ACTIVE IMAGINATION

A few people work through their Active Imagination in special modes. They may express their inner imagery through dance, by playing music, drawing, painting, sculpting, or speaking the dialogue out loud.

I once had a patient who was a dancer, and she could only express the events and dialogues in her imagination by *dancing* them. The first time she did that, it actually scared me speechless. She was acting out all the rawness, all the beauty, drama, struggle, and tragedy that went on in her inner life—all through her dance. She danced each character, acted out each role, portrayed animals, growled, grunted, shouted, fought, wept.

By the time her session was over I was crouched down, trying to hide in my chair. She said cheerfully, "Okay, Robert, you can come out now."

After each session she put into words for me what she had danced, what she had felt and seen in her imagination, and what it meant to her. This was helpful to me, since dance was, for me, a foreign language. Talking about it also helped her to make it more conscious.

If you use one of these other modes, such as dancing or painting or playing in a sand tray, to act out the imagination or record it, it is still good to do some writing. Writing always helps to focus and make it conscious. For most people, writing is the best and most accessible form.

THE PHYSICAL SETTING

Now that you have decided how you will record your imagination, you need to set up a room that is quiet and private enough that you can shut off the outside world for a while. You really cannot dialogue with your inner self if there are doorbells and telephones ringing every five minutes, children running through the room, dogs demanding to be fed or petted, and all of last month's unpaid bills sitting on the desk to distract you.

You have to be assertive enough to set aside a room and a block of time for yourself. Tell everyone in the house that you are not to be disturbed except for a nuclear blast or the Second Coming. You are entitled to that kind of freedom, privacy, and security. You need it in order to make your journey into the inner world.

You also need to be *alone*. No matter how intimate you may be with another person, it is usually impossible to spill out everything that is hidden in your secret, unconscious depths if you have someone else in the room who might wander over and look over your shoulder at what you are writing. If you feel like pacing the room, cursing, talking to some inner figure out loud, pounding on the wall, crying—you should be able to let out your raw feelings and emotions without worrying that someone is watching and listening to you.

There is also the temptation to start composing the Active Imagination so that it would sound nice and impressive for the other person if he or she happened to read it. It has to be clear that only *you* will ever read these pages; otherwise it will be very difficult to be honest in what you record.

Now that you have set the stage, found a private place to work, locked the door, and decided how you are going to write or type your Active Imagination, you are ready to begin.

Step One: The Invitation

> In mezzo del camin di nostra vita
> Mi ritrovai per una selva oscura
> Che la diritta via era smarrita
>
> E quanto a dir qualera e cosa dura
> Questa selva selvaggia . . .
>
> In the midpoint of this journey that is our life
> I found myself passing through a dark forest,
> The right path through which had disappeared.
>
> And what a hard thing it is to speak
> of that savage forest . . .
>
> —Dante, *Divine Comedy*

The first step in Active Imagination is to *invite* the creatures of the unconscious to come up to the surface and make contact with us. We invite the inner persons to start the dialogue.

How do we make this invitation? We begin by taking our minds off the external world around us and focusing on the imagination. We direct our inner eye to a place inside us, then we wait to see who will show up.

In the lines quoted above from Dante's *Divine Comedy*, we see how he set up the invitation. He went into his imagination and immediately found himself in a darkened forest. All the collective paths were eradicated: "The right path through it had disappeared." He had to struggle through the tangled undergrowth and make his own path of discovery.

There are a few great examples of Active Imagination in literature. The *Divina Commedia* is one of them. Wandering in the dark forest, Dante falls through a hole in the ground, and finds himself in the inner world. He is at the threshold of Hades. He meets the poet Virgil, who, as he discovers, was sent to him by the beautiful Beatrice. Virgil guides him and talks with him as they hike through the various levels of hell.

This is a classic example of how to begin Active Imagination.

Go to a place, describe it vividly and in detail so as to get yourself anchored there, and then see whom you encounter. In Dante's case, once he connected with Virgil and began walking, he met various people. Some of them were historical figures; some were people he had been personally acquainted with before they died. With each one he had an exchange of ideas or a clash of values.

At a certain point Virgil bows out and says that one greater than he will be Dante's guide for the rest of his journey. Then appears Beatrice, one of the great symbols of anima in all Western literature, who leads Dante to purgatory and paradise.

The *Commedia* is true Active Imagination. Dante tells his story in the first person. His ego lives through the entire experience, reacting, taking part in the events, dialoguing with the inner persons that he finds in his imagination. It is a spontaneous outpouring of Dante's own unconscious, mediated to us through his imagination. He deals with the great archetypal themes of loyalty and treason, virtue and evil, heaven and hell, life and death, that spring from the collective unconscious. They are common to all of us, but this was his version of the archetypal themes, his own experience of the universal leitmotivs, his own individual way of living out the evolution that each of us must make.

You don't need to write a great work of literature. In fact, if you started writing for other people's eyes it would probably distract you from living out your inner adventure honestly. But you do need to write your own episode, your own chapter in the universal *Divina Commedia* that is our common human life. In order to do this you can't copy Dante's version or someone else's. You must record what spontaneously flows through you from your own special corner of the collective unconscious.

For many people, this first step, the invitation, is a little difficult at first. They sit down at the typewriter, or with pen in hand, and find that their minds have gone blank.

If this happens, it may be that all you need is to have patience. Just wait, keep your mind focused on your imagination, and images will usually appear before long. If not, then you need to use one of the specific techniques that follow.

Sometimes it is hard to get something going. We may slam so many doors in the faces of our interior persons that, when we finally get around to opening the door, they don't come running out to greet us. If they do, they are likely to be angry and say, "Look, you have ignored me and slammed the door in my face so many times that, now that I have your attention, I have a few things to say to you!" But once you have invited, you have to take what comes.

To invite doesn't mean to *manage*. Everyone who begins this art has a lot of preconceived ideas about who *ought* to be there and what these inner characters *ought* to say. People expect to hear immediately noble speeches by the Great Mother or profound wisdom from an inner guru. These things often happen, but just as often we find ourselves looking at the depression we have refused to face, the sense of loneliness, emptiness, or inferiority we've always run from.

If this is what happens when you make your invitation, accept it. This negative material is the other side of your total reality. Now or later, you must dialogue with it. Jung said that it is exactly where you feel most frightened and most in pain that your greatest opportunity lies for personal growth.

With these basic principles in mind, we can look now at some specific approaches you can use for making your invitation.

WAITING ON ALERT

Perhaps the purest form of Active Imagination is that in which you simply clear your mind, go to your imagination, and wait to see who will appear. This is the approach that Von Franz calls "emptying the ego-mind." We clear the mind of all thoughts of the external world and simply wait, with an alert and attentive attitude, to see who or what will appear.

Sometimes this approach may require great patience and concentration. Nothing may appear for some time. What does come up may seem insignificant or unworthy to your ego-mind, causing you to reject it out of hand. If you focus your mind long enough you will usually find that some image is waiting in the wings, ready to come on stage and present itself to your attention. When this figure does appear, you should not stand in judgment, give in to your prejudices, or reject it. It is best to assume that it has something to say that is relevant.

A figure from your dream from last night may rise up, and you may find that this image wants to continue where it left off in the dream. Or an image may appear that you have never seen before. You may wonder who this is and why he or she has appeared in your imagination. So the simplest invitation is the most obvious: "Who are you? What do you want? What do you have to say?" Your dialogue begins.

I have said that this is probably the "purest" form of Active Imagination because the ego does not choose whom you will dialogue with or what will rise up into the imagination. You present an attitude of complete receptiveness to whatever appears, with no preconditions or expectations attached.

HOW TO START

Many people are not suited to the method of pure receptiveness, or clearing the ego-mind. They find it very difficult to get their imagination launched by merely focusing the mind and waiting. They may just draw a complete blank for long periods of time.

I believe that in these cases it is correct to "prime the pump"— that is, to do something specific and deliberate to get the flow of imagination going. We will now look at several legitimate ways that you can do this.

One precaution must be observed: Once you have found the image and started the inner dialogue, you must relinquish control. Once the invitation is made and the image appears, you can't dictate the focus of your imagination and you can't push it in any particular direction.

1. USING YOUR FANTASIES

Harnessing fantasy is a way of converting passive fantasy into Active Imagination. In its simplest form, you look at the fantasies that have been going through your mind today and you choose an image, an inner person, or a situation. Then you go to that place and that person and use it as the starting place for Active Imagination. Participate in the fantasy, enter into dialogue with the characters, record what is done and said, and thereby convert this passive fantasy into genuine Active Imagination.

This approach to Active Imagination is especially helpful when a person has too much fantasy material. The Active Imagination will reduce the quantity and intensity of the fantasy by relieving the pressure from below. When you have a recurring fantasy that stays in your mind all day, it indicates that there is some inner problem that needs to be worked through. When a huge number of fantasies flood your mind, it often means that you haven't been giving enough attention to the unconscious. It compensates your imbalance toward the outer world by flooding you with fantasy—which forces you into a kind of involuntary inner life.

In these situations, Jung said, you can take the subject of your fantasy and start a conscious dialogue with its images. Instead of passively watching the same fantasy repeat itself over and over in your mind, you carry the material forward in Active Imagination. You establish a dialogue among the different parts of yourself that are concerned and bring the conflict to a resolution. You convert the fantasy into consciousness.

Remember that fantasies are excellent divining rods. If a fantasy is running through the back of your mind today, you can safely assume that it is expressing, in symbolic form, one of the main dynamics, conflicts, or areas where psychic energy is concentrated in you. If you go to that fantasy and take it as a starting point for Active Imagination, you will be automatically focused on an inner subject that is immediate, relevant, and important.

So there are two important things you can accomplish by learning to harness passive fantasy and turn it into Active Imagination. First, it will help you to make your *invitation* when you have "gone dry," when no images come up, your mind is blank, and you can't seem to get your imagination started. Second, when you find that you have a stream of fantasies that overwhelms you, it is an excellent way to focus on a fantasy, bring it up to the surface, and "live it out" consciously through Active Imagination. Instead of letting the stream of fantasy repeat itself wastefully, or trying to act it out externally, you make it conscious on the level where it belongs—the level of imagination.

2. VISITING SYMBOLIC PLACES

One very simple way of making your invitation is to *go to a place* in your imagination, and start exploring to see whom you meet there. Usually when you do this, your imagination will take you to the inner place where you need to go and connect you to the inner persons that you need to meet.

Many peole fall into the habit, without realizing it, of returning to a special place in their imagination. Remember the man who goes off on adventures with the Renaissance cavalier? Notice that he has the custom of always returning to the same *bridge* in his imagination. At that bridge the Renaissance man always comes to take him off into the inner world.

For me, the seashore is a magical place that often appears in my dreams. When I don't know how to start my Active Imagination, I frequently go to the seashore in my mind and start walking. Inevitably something happens or someone appears, and the imagination is launched. There have been a few days when I walked and walked, and almost nothing happened; sometimes you can grow weary walking. But generally, if you go to the inner place and search, you will find someone waiting for you.

I had a patient years ago who had a terrible time getting started in his Active Imagination. Nothing ever seemed to happen to him in his external life, and the same dull quality carried over into his imagination. He was an absolute blank. So I told him to go to the beach, as I do, and start walking, and look around and see who he would meet.

The next week he returned and said: "Yes. I walked on the beach. But no one wanted to talk to me. Nothing happened."

So I got mildly upset: "Look! Something *has* to happen. You walk on the beach long enough and your feet will get blisters. You'll have to go to the hospital. You'll fall in love with the nurse and get married. Something will happen. Now go do it!"

The following week he returned, looked at me with his absolutely serious, deadpan expression, and said: "The nurse wasn't any good, so I didn't marry her." But at least he got started.

Your inner place may be a grove in the jungle, an Arcadian meadow with Pan lurking in the shadows, or a monastery cell. You can find the place within you where the energy is, and you can learn how to find your way back to it. Going to your inner place becomes your way of inviting the inner world.

3. USING PERSONIFICATIONS

Let us go back in our minds to the woman who was obsessed with painting her house. You may remember that she made her *invitation* by personifying the obsessive feelings. She looked for an image that would represent the one inside who was possessed.

She started by talking to the one who seemed obsessed. At first it was like talking to the air around her. Then she heard a voice in her imagination that, in turn, became an image that she could see:

E: What is happening here? I've been taken over by an unknown force. I can't sleep for the barrage of hues before my eyes. What are you doing? What do you want? Who are you?

(Voice): (Sounds like a feminine voice in my imagination.) The colors are so lovely. See the interplay. See how they evoke different aspects of nature. These, in particular, go so well with the wood tones of the bookshelves—

E: Excuse me . . .

This provides you with another way of priming the pump. If you have some affect that is following you around and dogging your steps, some mood that you can't shake off, this gives you a strong hint as to where you should go to start your dialogue with the unconscious. Go to the one inside you who is obsessed, depressed, or in some other mood.

Go into your imagination and say: "Why is the one inside me who is depressed today? Where are you? What do you look like? Please take some form I can see and come up and talk with me. I want to know who you are and what you want."

4. DIALOGUING WITH DREAM FIGURES

One of the earliest uses that Jung found for Active Imagination was as a means of *extending dreams*. If a dream is not resolved, or you keep getting the same dream over and over again, you can extend the dream out through imagination and bring it to a resolution. This is a legitimate use of imagination, since the dream and the imagination come from the same source in the unconscious.

This, in turn, provides another way to make an invitation. One goes back to the dream in imagination and enters into dialogue with the characters there. One can pick out a specific person in the dream that one feels the need to talk with. One can speak specifically with a single dream figure or return to the situation in the dream and take up the whole encounter where the dream left off. You can effectively *continue* the dream and interact with it by extending it out into your Active Imagination.

In this form, Active Imagination becomes a valuable addition to your dream work. It allows you to go to a dream where you have been left hanging, where the situation has not been resolved, to develop the inner situation that the dream presented. It allows you to "continue the story," go through the next step the dream is leading toward, and bring the whole issue to a resolution.

So when you find yourself wanting to do Active Imagination but can't seem to get started or find a starting point, go to a recent dream. Not only will it help you to get the Active Imagination flowing, it will transform your relationship to your dream and your relationship to the inner person, because you will be adding your conscious participation to the dream.

ACTIVE IMAGINATION ILLUSTRATIONS

Before we move on to the second step, I will give you three examples of experiences in either extending a dream with Active Imagination or using a dream person for dialoguing.

Our first example comes from Jung. This was one of the earliest uses that he made of Active Imagination. Jung discovered the seeds of some of his most profound and far-reaching insights into the nature of the psyche by going to an inner person, whom he called Philemon and who first appeared in a dream, and doing Active Imagination with him.

Soon after this fantasy another figure rose out of the Unconscious. He developed out of the Elijah figure. I called him Philemon. Philemon was a pagan and brought with him an Egypto-Hellenistic atmosphere with a Gnostic coloration. His figure first appeared to me in the following dream:

There was a blue sky, like the sea, covered not by clouds but by flat brown clods of earth. It looked as if the clods were breaking apart and the blue water of the sea were becoming visible between them. But the water was the blue sky. Suddenly there appeared from the right a winged being sailing across the sky. I saw that it was an old man with the horns of a bull. He held a bunch of four keys, one of which he clutched as if he were about to open a lock. He had the wings of the kingfisher with its characteristic colors.

. . . Philemon and other figures of my fantasies brought home to me the crucial insight that there are things in the psyche which I do not produce, but which produce themselves and have their own life. Philemon represented a force which was not myself. In my fantasies I held conversations with him, and he said things which I had not consciously thought. For I observed clearly that it was he who spoke, not I. He said I treated thoughts as if I generated them myself, but in his view thoughts were like animals in the forest. . . . It was he who taught me psychic objectivity, the reality of the psyche. Through him the distinction was clarified between myself and the object of my thought. . . .

Psychologically, Philemon represented superior insight. He was a mysterious figure to me. At times he seemed to me quite real, as if he were a living personality. I went walking up and down the garden with him, and to me he was what the Indians call a guru. (*MDR*, pp. 182–83)

There is a seemingly endless variety of relationships that can be established with dream persons if you will go to them in Active Imagination. And you can confirm in your own experience that you begin to change inwardly in response to the dialogues and experiences that you pass through with these inner persons. If there is a terrible conflict with a dream figure during your dream, you can spend many sessions of Active Imagination with that person, working out the conflict and reaching an understanding. If, like Jung, you discover a wise, prophetic old man or woman in your dream, you can go back to that dream person regularly to ask for wisdom and counsel.

A long time ago I dreamed that I was sitting in my study, behaving myself and doing whatever one does in one's study. Suddenly, a lion walked in. It terrified me. I tried everything I could to get the lion out of the study. I pushed, I ordered, I demanded, I made a big noise that frightened me more than the lion; I twisted his tail. But there the dream ended. I was still terrified, and the lion wouldn't leave. As you can see, this is a completely unsatisfactory conclusion for a dream. There was no resolution of the problem.

So I took the dream into Active Imagination. In my imagination I started up exactly where the dream had left off. I immediately got frightened all over again; the hair went up on the back of my neck, and chills went down my spine—all of which means that it was high-quality Active Imagination. I was there in my feelings. It felt to me as though I had a physical lion in my physical study and my head might be bitten off. My heart pounded, I shook, and I broke out in a cold sweat.

I did four different sessions of Active Imagination on that dream before it dawned on me that the lion wasn't hurting me! One is so stupid with one's own interior things. Anyone else would have said within thirty seconds: "Look, the lion isn't hurting you. Why twist his tail? Maybe he has something to say. Maybe he is an important part of you that you need to accept." But it took four sessions of imagination—dedicated to trying to *get rid* of the creature—before it dawned on me that he probably belonged with me and I needed to integrate him into my life.

The imagination was so strong that I couldn't cut it off. Every time I went into my study to work, the imagination would start up again, and there would be the spirit-lion, prowling around the study. Every time I tried to do some work at my desk, he would come over and lick me, start sniffing at the typewriter, or growl out the window and distract me.

I started talking with him: "Who are you? What are you here for? Look what you are doing to my study. I can't get any work done around here with you breathing down my neck. Anyway, you scare the hell out of me, even if you are a dream lion. Why don't you go outside and find some other lions or something? Lions don't belong in the house, and they don't belong in my civilized, respectable, daily routine."

I got used to him. But it took many weeks for me to come to some kind of accord with that interior content in myself that chose to portray itself as a lion. It is a very powerful, even frightening, part of myself, so the more clearly I saw *who* that was, what part of me it was, the more scared I became at the implications. It took a lot of work to be able to face it.

Finally, after many, many sessions of Active Imagination, one day the lion went over to a particular place in my study, sat down on his back haunches, and became a bronze sculpture. In his right paw, which he held out, was a book. And I read the most amazing things in that book.

He has stayed there ever since. Occasionally I go in imagination back to that place in the interior study to see if he is still there. He is. And the book is still there, always opened to a page with important information.

Our final example in this chapter is the experience of a young woman who had a short dream about her husband and her brother. Since the dream "left her hanging," so to speak, she decided to go to the persons in the dream in Active Imagination and see if she could get the issues ironed out. With this example we have the advantage of a transcript of the actual word-for-word dialogue that she did in her imagination.

You will recognize this dream. It is the first dream we looked at in this book. We have already seen how the dreamer drew meanings from it through dream work. Now we also see how she used her dream to launch Active Imagination.

Dream

I am looking for my car keys. I realize my husband has them. Then I realize that my brother has borrowed my car and has not returned it. I see both of them and I call to them. They do not seem to hear me. Then a disheveled young man, like a "renegade," gets into my car and drives off. I feel extremely frustrated, helpless, abandoned, upset.

Note from the Dreamer

I decided to do an Active Imagination because there was no resolution to the problem in the dream, and I always feel that that is a clear invitation from the unconscious to work with imagination. I felt the dream showed I was in bad relationship to my inner masculine side. I had no communication. My collective way, the car, was being taken away, but there was no solution to the problem. I set up dialogue with the three men in the dream, but I changed the images so they wouldn't look exactly like my physical brother and husband, so that the imagination would not work "magic" on the external husband and brother. I dialogued with the archetypal, generic "husband" and "brother."

I: Why are you doing this to me?
        (To H and B) You've both broken promises.

H & B: (Both silent. They won't talk. The renegade turns his back on me and faces away.)

I: Please. Why won't you talk to me? Please speak. Why did you take my car away in the dream? Why did you leave me alone? What is going on?

H & B: (They look at each other. I see the "husband" has the keys in his hand.)

I: You are ignoring me; yet you've clearly done something
        to get my attention. What do you want?
            (long silence)

I: Please don't ignore me. It hurts. I need to talk with you.

H: You have been ignoring us. Besides, you don't need keys.

I: I can't drive without them.

B: You don't need a car.

I: I don't understand.

H: (Tosses keys to B and says:) If you are going to act like
        superwoman all the time, why don't you *fly* where you
        need to go?

I: (Now I feel very wounded. I begin to understand his
        meaning. I have been far too busy, trying to do too
        much, inflated. I feel how sad—empty is more apt—
        empty I am beneath all this striving.)

H: You act as if you don't need us, as if you don't need *any-
        thing*. That's why we have been so distant.

I: I can see how I've been alienated from both of you. No
        wonder I've become so strained lately. I'm sorry. I let
        myself get overwhelmed by work, and I went completely
        unconscious.

            (Now I have a sense of who the "renegade" is. He
        turns to face me.)

            (Speaking to Renegade:) You are the runaway energy
        in me. You say yes to tasks that seem reasonable, produc-
        tive, worthwhile, and by an arbitrary standard they may
        be so. But they are not what I *want*. I see now: You are
        the one who gets in the car and just drives off with me.
        You set up all this forward motion.

            But it isn't what I want, and it isn't what is right for
        me. As I look at all I am doing I see that the writing proj-
        ect can wait. And I no longer want to teach the continu-
        ation class. The other classes are fine, but one less will
        make my life my own again.

R: The writing project is a good one. It could be significant
        to other people. Besides, you have already said you were
        interested.

I: I made no commitments. You make it seem as if waiting
        would be catastrophic. It isn't so.

R: Well, omitting the class will disappoint the students. They specifically *requested* it in order to help with the field placements. You will lose credibility if you back out . . .

I: Many people depend on me, but I am not indispensable. Someone else can teach it. The students will learn from having another point of view.

       (I am feeling increasingly more balanced, more myself. I don't like the anxiety of refusing these requests, yet there are obviously more demands than can be met. I dislike even more the feeling of "too-muchness," of doing things unconsciously, of feeling disconnected and automatic.)

I: Look, I like my work, but when I allow you to dictate to me I feel less and less joy in what I do. I forgot to notice the difference between what is practical and what holds meaning. I am not backing out. I am waking up. I am choosing.

       (I hear a group of starlings in the acacia tree outside my window. Their voices are distinct and fresh. I hadn't noticed them before. How could I have missed it? I fall into quietness and thank the starlings for calling me to attention. After some time I note that the three figures before me have been transformed. There is one man, a beloved figure from former dreams. We are attuned in the silence and remain so for some time.)

This example shows us how a short, unresolved dream situation can be transformed by extending it into Active Imagination. How quickly and directly she found the main application of the dream! By going to the three dream figures and asking them to talk with her, she effectively started the dream all over again at the point where it had left off. But the dream took on a new element at that point because she added her conscious participation to it. Instead of merely watching the dream, she entered into it and began to play a conscious role in it.

Even with the advantage of knowing with whom she wanted to speak, she still had some difficulty with the *invitation*: At first these dream characters didn't want to speak. But by persistently keeping after them and letting them know that she was ready to talk and to listen, she pulled them out of their resentment and got the dialogue going.

From these examples, please find encouragement to go to your own dreams and use them as starting points for making your invitation to the unconscious. Use this method as a way of continuing your own dream until you make the evolution and gain the consciousness that is yours.

Step Two: The Dialogue

You have invited the unconscious; the images have risen up into your imagination. Now you are ready to begin the dialogue.

Making a dialogue is mostly a matter of giving yourself over to the imagination and letting it flow. There are various principles we can follow, but moving the experience ahead consists, more than anything else, in letting the inner figures have a life of their own.

As a practical matter you say or do whatever comes into your mind that feels appropriate and ethical. If a figure appears in the imagination and seems to have nothing to say at first, one may get the conversation going by asking who he or she is. Ask what the person wants, what the person would like to talk about, would like to do. It is better to ask questions than to lecture or start making pronouncements, because the basic attitude you want to show is a *willingness to listen.*

If an inner figure does something, write it down; then do or say whatever your reaction is in response. Often an inner person will try to draw you into some activity, take you somewhere, lead you off on a path or a journey. If it seems right to you, then do it, and record what happens along the way. If you feel that it is wrong to follow the person, or you don't like the activity or involvement that the inner person suggests, you have the right to say so. You have the right to refuse and to state your reasons. That, in turn, will often lead to a heated discussion of the conflict between this inner person and what you think you want—or don't want, or don't approve of, or are afraid of. All this is excellent material for the Active Imagination: The dialogue has begun, and the different parts of the self are learning from each other.

If you find that an inner character won't speak, it is legitimate to "prime the pump." You can initiate an exchange just as you might if you were stuck with a guest who was shy and uncommunicative. Ask questions, express your feelings. If you are afraid of the person who has come up, say so. If the person reminds you of an experience you had, or a dream, or someone in the outer world that you know, tell the person about it.

Probably nothing gets the dialogue going as quickly or on as deep a level as does an expression of feelings. When you let your feelings out and invite your inner person to do the same, it usually constellates the exchange very directly. This is because feelings are mostly concerned with *values*: who or what we love and appreciate, what we are afraid of, what we feel is dishonest or illegitimate, what we desire for ourselves and others. And values, we find, are the mainsprings of our human lives.

It is extremely important to write down everything as it happens and everything that is said. Writing protects you from wandering off into passive fantasies that creep in from the edges of the mind. It helps you to concentrate more and experience more deeply. The physical writing etches the experience more vividly in the conscious mind.

CONVERSING WITH ONE IMAGE

In order to do a true act of imagination, it is necessary to stick with the image that we start with, stay with the situation until there is some kind of resolution. Once one has encountered a particular image or started a dialogue with it, it is important to continue from there and not allow oneself to be distracted by other images or fantasy material that may jump into the mind and compete with the Active Imagination.

If you allow your mind to flit from image to image and situation to situation, you will only put yourself through a meaningless series of starts and stops, none of which will lead anywhere. If your ego is genuinely going to the inner figures and interacting with them, then there will be a continuous, coherent experience with the original figures. Don't sit passively while your mind flits from one image to another, from one film clip to another.

Active Imagination is a complete experience, one that has a beginning, a middle, and an end. Like a dream, it usually produces a statement of a problem, a period of interaction with the problem and the different viewpoints on the subject, and finally a resolution of the conflict or the issue. This may take place in one session, or it may require a series of sessions that continue for days or even years.

You can get a perspective on this by remembering the examples we have already given. The first was the dialogue between a woman and her inner Japanese artist. In that dialogue one can easily identify the point where the problem was raised, right at the beginning. There followed a long conversation in which the alternatives were spelled out that might be solutions to the problem. Finally, at the end of the dialogue, there was a resolution. This was not the last conversation with the Japanese artist. But already within this one session, we find a resolution of the basic issue.

By contrast, consider the example of the man who was led off on his mythical journey to help the Queen who was in distress. In this session of Active Imagination the problem has been stated: There are evil forces at work in the land, people being hurt. All this is being blamed on the innocent queen. As the man sets off on his journey with his guide, he does what he can to begin to heal the land by healing the little girl. But his adventure has only begun, there is more work to do. In fact, this particular Active Imagination has gone on for years, and still continues.

PARTICIPATING WITH YOUR FEELINGS

Full participation is the essence of Active Imagination. All the things we have said about the distinction between Active Imagination and passive fantasy are particularly important at this stage. It is vital to join in as a complete partner in the exchange. One may make suggestions, initiate, ask questions, argue, object—everything one would do in any exchange between equals.

The most important aspect of this is to be present in your *feelings* and participate with your feelings. One must sense that it is real, that it is actually *happening*—even though it is inside rather than outside. If you are detached from it, or just feel that it is nothing but a fantasy you are watching from a safe distance, there is no real experience. If one is not really participating with the feeling side, it is not true Active Imagination.

A good example of being present in your feelings is the woman in the example who dreamed that two male figures, who resembled her husband and her brother, were ignoring her. What kind of feelings did she have when she went to them in Active Imagination? She was furious, she was hurt, she was indignant—and she actually felt all that. Her feelings and her emotions were there in the exchange with these two inner persons, and it was her feelings, finally, that they responded to.

One can usually tell whether a person is doing real Active Imagination by the feeling responses that come out. If the normal human reaction to the situation in the imagination would be anger, fear, or intense joy, but none of these feelings are present, then I know the person is detached from the proceedings, just watching from a distance, not really participating, not taking it seriously.

We must participate completely. There is, however, one line that should not be crossed. We must not stray from the zone of participation into the zone of *control*. In Active Imagination we cannot exert control over the inner persons or over what is happening. We have to let the imagination flow where it will, let the experience develop, without trying to determine in advance what is going to happen, what is going to be said, what is going to be done.

Sometimes it is hard to see the difference between fully participating and trying to control. You can draw a good analogy from your dialogues with external people. When you are in a conversation with someone, courtesy and respect lead you to give the other person "equal time." We try not to dominate the conversation; we don't flood the other person with a stream of opinions so as to cut off his or her chance to express a viewpoint. The same rules of courtesy, restraint, and respect apply when we dialogue with the citizens of the inner world.

Sometimes what your inner person is saying sounds stupid, primitive, or nonsensical. Or it rubs you so completely against the grain that you get angry. Still, you must let it be said. Try dropping control for once; stop trying to make the inner figures sound intelligent or sensible according to your ego's standards, and let them be whoever or whatever they are.

To give up control means to relinquish your preconceptions about what should happen, what should be said, what message or meaning ought to come out of all this. In fact, you should not be thinking about what it *means* at all, at this stage, because that would lead you into trying to stage-manage the experience to come out with the right "messages." We need to forbear imposing the ego's expectations on the proceedings. We need to give up the *ought-to* mentality and, instead, let flow what *is*—the feelings, conflicts, and personalities that truly live in us below the surface.

LEARNING TO LISTEN

Active Imagination is, more than anything, a process of listening.

Not all dialogue or interaction with your inner persons will be through words. There are sessions of Active Imagination in which the entire experience takes place through actions, through seeing and doing. It is still a dialogue, but a dialogue without words. More often than not, however, there will be spoken dialogue. In either case, we have to learn to listen.

Often we have only experienced these parts of ourselves who now come up as images in our imagination as enemies—as carriers of slothful resistance, neurosis, unproductive vices, immaturity. That is how they look to the ego. But now, if we are going to set up an exchange in place of the habitual, lifelong war we have fought, we have to begin to listen.

After so many years of ignoring these parts of ourselves, seeing them as the inferior characteristics in our personalities, we find that they have some very unpleasant things to tell us when we finally listen. It is no surprise that some inner person tells me what a tyrant I have been over the years, how I have shoved my ego's attitudes down the throat of the unconscious.

One must be willing to say: "Who are you? What do you have to say? I will listen to you. You may have the floor for this entire hour if you want; you may use any language you want. I am here to listen."

This requires a formidable realignment of attitude for most of us. If there is something in yourself that you see as a weakness, a defect, a terrible obstruction to a productive life, you nevertheless have to stop approaching that part of yourself as "the bad guy." For once, during Active Imagination, you must try to listen to that "inferior" being as though he or she were the voice of wisdom. If our depressions or weaknesses come to us in personified form, we need to honor those characteristics as part of the total self.

It is awesome and frightening to take your sense of inferiority, guilt, or remorse, put that part of you in the witness box, and say: "You have every privilege. You are the one who bears witness to that which I neither know nor understand. You may say whatever you wish, at whatever length. You will be respected and honored. And what you say will be recorded." But it is from this that the true power of Active Imagination rises: We learn to listen to the ones whom we have kept mute. We learn to honor those whom we have dishonored.

LEARNING TO REPLY

When we have learned to listen, we must also learn to reply—to contribute our own information, viewpoint, and values.

When people first learn to honor the voice of the unconscious and to take it seriously, there is often a tendency to go overboard and decide that "this ego knows nothing." There is a tendency to take everything the inner figures say as final authority. This would be just as foolish and one-sided as our previous ego-centered approach. Just as the ego needs to balance its viewpoints by going to the unconscious, so also does the unconscious need to be balanced by the attitudes of the conscious mind.

Remember Jung's observation: He said that the ego's relationship to the huge unconscious is like that of a tiny cork floating in the ocean. We often feel like that. We feel like a cork that is being tossed about in the ocean of life, completely at the mercy of the waves and storms that push and pull us. We seem to have little control or power over anything.

Jung continued his analogy with a startling thing: The cork is nevertheless morally equal to the ocean, because it has the power of consciousness! Although the ego is small, it has this peculiar power of awareness that we call consciousness, and that special, concentrated power gives it a position that is as necessary, as strong, and as valuable as the seemingly infinite richness of the unconscious. The little cork can talk back to the ocean, and has a viewpoint to contribute, one without which the evolution of consciousness cannot proceed. The ego can talk back, and this makes the dialogue one between equals.

The ego's capacity for consciousness gives it the power, the right, and even the duty to wrestle with the great unconscious on equal terms and to work out a synthesis of values.

NOT MANIPULATING

One of the most important laws of this second step in Active Imagination is that you never work with a prepared script. You don't know what is going to happen until it happens.

You may know how you feel about something; you may know what you have to say to the inner person; you may know who you are looking for when you go into your imagination. But you don't know what the other person is going to say until he or she says it. You don't know what the inner people are going to do until they do it. You have the right to call out your anima, your animus, or your shadow figures, but you don't have the right to plan what they are going to say, and you don't have the right to dominate them once they appear.

At its best, Active Imagination is a life of surprises, a life that is given over to the unexpected. We make no plan or script. We simply begin, and then let come what will. Whatever flows spontaneously out of the unconscious, without manipulation, without guidance or control, is the stuff of Active Imagination.

We need to grasp this clearly because there are now so many systems around that can be confused with Active Imagination but are completely distinct from it. The main difference is that they work with a prepared script; everything is determined in advance.

These systems are sometimes called "guided imagery," "creative imagery," or by something else. What they all have in common is that everything is *predetermined*. You decide in advance what is going to happen in your imagination. The ego decides what it is trying to get out of the unconscious and prepares a script. The idea is to "program" the unconscious so that it will do what the ego wants it to do.

In one system, the whole avowed purpose of using the imagery is to *get what you want*. You close your eyes and visualize the new car or the new job or the house in the country that you want, and you use the power of visualization to get these things. In another system, you attempt to have a better attitude about yourself by using self-imagery. You visualize yourself as you would like to be—slender, attractive, effective, efficient, or whatever. By the use of self-imagery one attempts to become the idealized person that the ego has decided it would like one to be.

The problem with these approaches to imagery is that it is the ego that does all the deciding. The unconscious is seen as a sort of stupid animal that has no viewpoint of its own, no wisdom to contribute. The whole point of the exchange is to train the unconscious to do what the ego wants. The ego's decisions may seem to be good ones; the problem is that the unconscious is not consulted in making them.

Active Imagination starts out from a completely different idea about the unconscious. We affirm that the unconscious has its own wisdom, its own viewpoints, and that they are often as balanced, as realistic, as those of the ego-mind. The purpose of Active Imagination is not to "program" the unconscious, but to *listen* to the unconscious. And, if you do listen, the unconscious, in turn, will listen to you.

If you have decided that you want to accomplish some big project, and you find that the unconscious is setting up resistance against it, you should not react by trying to "program" the unconscious to agree with your ideas. Instead, you should go to the unconscious and find the one who is causing the paralysis, the resistance, or the depression, and find out *why*. If you do this, you are often surprised to find out that the unconscious has very good reasons for disagreeing with your project or your goals.

Perhaps you are about to go off on a big inflation or obsession, trying to achieve something that is actually impossible. Your unconscious is likely to resist and try to bring you to your senses so that you scale down your project to something that is within your resources and capacities. Or your plans may mean doing permanent damage to your family life, your marriage, relationships, or friendships; the unconscious may send you physical symptoms, a feeling of depression or paralysis, in order to prevent you from going off on a tangent that would destroy something vital in your life.

Active Imagination begins with the principle that you must respect the unconscious and realize that it has something valuable to contribute; therefore, the dialogue must be one between two intelligent equals who respect each other. It can't be a case of one trying to "program" the other.

This is why, in Active Imagination, there is no script. You don't follow a planned course. You don't put words in the mouths of those you meet. You don't decide in advance what the goal is. You don't set up a purpose and then try to manipulate the unconscious into going along with it.

Historically there are some legitimate and fine uses that have been made of guided imagery. One example is the *Greater Exercises of Saint Ignatius of Loyola*. This is a series of meditations on the life of Christ that uses a prescribed guided visualization each day. Jung gave a series of lectures years ago in Switzerland in which he used the *Greater Exercises* to show the differences between Active Imagination and guided imagery at its best.

In this guided imagery you go, for example, to the Via Dolorosa. It is the day of the Crucifixion, and you are there, present in your imagination. You smell the dust, sweat, and blood. You hear the jeering of the crowd. You see the crown of thorns, the cross, the blood flowing. You feel the sharp stones beneath your feet, the sun beating down on you as you move with the crowd toward Golgotha.

In this way, for those who adopted Loyola's meditations, the events of the life of Christ were made so vivid—smelling, feeling, touching, hurting—that they became actual, immediate experience. This sort of guided imagery is good if it truly serves your religious purposes. It was geared mainly to the medieval mentality, but much of that mentality still lives on in us and we can honor it.

But Jung said it would be better for us if we could go in Active Imagination, walk on our own Via Dolorosa, and find out what is there within our own individual selves. It would not be predetermined by anyone or anything except the reality of what lives inside us. It would not be prescribed by authority or tradition. You might find yourself walking on the stones of an ancient way, as did Loyola, or you might find yourself walking the deck of a yacht, if that is where your inner path leads. Of one thing you can be sure: Ultimately every road is a Via Dolorosa, for it leads us into the issues and conflicts that every person must pass through, sometimes painfully and with heroic spirit, sometimes with sacrifice, in order to be initiated into the realm of consciousness.

If you have a modern mentality, you must find your own path. *Go your own way*, which is both terrifying and exhilarating. No one can tell you any longer *the* way, because there is no longer one prescribed way, but only *a* way—*your* way, which is as valid as any other as long as you live it honestly.

Much of the artificial loneliness of your life will evaporate if you realize that your way is merely *a* way—one way among many, yet unique and distinct from all others, springing from your own nature, a way that is inborn, not made, and waits to be discovered.

For each of us, that path is a solitary one, for ultimately we must walk it alone. No one else can tell us which final direction it should take, and no one else can walk it for us.

If you will walk in this way, Active Imagination is your proper path.

Step Three: The Values

So far we have seen how to invite the figures from the unconscious and how to enter into a dialogue with them. But this is not enough. We must also take an ethical stance. It is our job, as conscious human beings, to introduce the ethical element into the proceedings.

Once the imaginative process is launched, once the primordial, instinctual forces are invited to come up to the surface and be heard, some limits have to be set. It is the conscious ego, guided by a sense of ethics, that must set limits in order to protect the imaginative process from becoming inhuman or destructive or going off into extremes.

Jung took the audacious point of view that humanity holds a specific role in creation: to contribute the act of consciousness and the point of view of morality, in its highest sense. We are surrounded by a universe that is awesome and beautiful, but its forces behave in a way that is amoral. They are not concerned, as we are, with the specifically human values of justice, fairness, protection of the defenseless, service to our fellow humans, the keeping intact of the fabric of practical life. It is we who have to introduce these values into the world around us. And since the creatures who arise in our Active Imagination are often, for all practical purposes, personifications of the impersonal forces of nature, it is we who must bring the ethical, humane, and practical elements into Active Imagination.

Jung also observed that there is no development of consciousness, in the human sense, without ethical conflict. Consciousness always involves ethical confrontations: We become aware of the conflicting values, attitudes, and paths of conduct that are open to us and find that we must make moral choices.

All these principles find their way into Active Imagination. As the inner figures present themselves, as the different attitudes and possibilities rise to the surface, inevitably we have to take an ethical stance in order to strike a balance among conflicting values.

It is equally a grave mistake to think that it is enough to gain some understanding of the images and that knowledge can here make a halt. Insight into them must be converted into an ethical obligation. Not to do so is to fall prey to the power principle, and this produces dangerous effects which are destructive not only to others but even to the knower. The images of the unconscious place a great responsibility upon a man. Failure to understand them, or a shirking of ethical responsibility, deprives him of his wholeness and imposes a painful fragmentariness on his life. (Jung, *MDR*, p. 192)

Jung told of a young man who dreamed that his girlfriend slid into an icy lake and was drowning beneath the water. Jung said, in effect, that the man could not just sit and let the cold forces of fate kill the inner feminine. He advised the man to go into Active Imagination, get something to pull her out of the water, build a fire for her, get some dry clothes for her, and save her life. This is the ethical, moral, and human thing to do. It is as much the ego's duty to bring this sense of responsibility to the creatures of the inner world as it is for us to tend to the welfare of our fellow humans in the outside world. It is the health of our own, inner selves that is at stake.

I recall a case in which an inner archetypal figure demanded absolute control over a woman's life, at the expense of her feminine nature. The woman was doing analysis with me, and her Active Imagination was mostly with a very powerful and wise masculine figure. He gave her good information, excellent insights, but he also tried to argue her out of some of her basic instincts as a woman. He was trying to take over more and more of her life at the expense of her essential character.

One day she was doing Active Imagination, and he suddenly said to her: "Give me your purse and your keys. From now on I am taking over." And, in her imagination, she did what she was told. She turned over her purse and her keys.

As she read this episode to me, I jumped to my feet: "No way will you give him your purse and keys! That symbolizes all your resources and complete control of your life. If you do that you will abdicate your rightful role and turn your entire consciousness over to only one part of yourself. You can't do that, no matter how wise or 'right' he seems to be. Only *you* can run your own life; you can't turn that role over to anyone else.

"Now, you have to do it over again: Go back and tell him that you are taking your purse and keys back. Tell him that you will listen to him, respect him, and consider what he says—but you cannot turn your whole life over to him. Tell him that you need to think for your own self and make your own decisions."

After my outburst, the woman did as I advised. She went back in Active Imagination and explained things to this powerful masculine figure. He understood the principle; he agreed; and he immediately gave her back the purse and keys.

Unfortunately, about a year later, after she had stopped analysis, this woman did turn herself over completely to her power drive. She let the power aspect of this masculine presence take over completely in her inner world. She went off on an inflation. She became a know-it-all, lectured everyone, and tried to dominate every situation.

This is an example of what happens when you allow yourself to go off on an inflation, be possessed by an archetype, and lose the independent position of your ego. How is making this choice an ethical problem? Whenever you allow one part of you to take over and subjugate all your other instincts and values, it is inherently destructive. Inevitably your conduct and your treatment of other people will be off balance.

Our word *ethics*, and our concept of ethical behavior, is derived from the Greek word that meant "proper conduct." It is instructive that this word was in turn derived from the Greek *ethos*, meaning the "essential character or spirit" of a person or people. *Ethics*, therefore, in its deepest sense, means the personal standard of conduct that accords with an individual's true inner character.

Ethics is a principle of unity and consistency. People who behave ethically are those who make an honest effort to conform their behavior to their values. If one's conduct is grossly at odds with one's essential character, it always reflects a fragmentation of the personality. As Jung said, "A shirking of ethical responsibility . . . deprives him of his wholeness and imposes a painful fragmentariness on his life."

From what we have said so far, we can summarize three specific elements involved in preserving the ethical aspect of Active Imagination:

First, you add the ethical element by holding out for the attitudes and conduct that are consistent with your character and your deepest values.

Second, ethical balance requires that we not let one archetype or one part of ourselves take over at the expense of the others. We can't sacrifice essential values in order to pursue one narrow urge or goal.

Third, we must nurture and preserve the specifically human values that serve human life, that keep practical daily life going, and that keep our human relationships alive.

The great powers of the collective unconscious are so overpowering that we can be suddenly swept away by a flood of primitive energy that seizes the conscious mind—an energy that races toward its instinctual goal, heedless of the effect that it may have on ordinary human life or on the people around you.

Inevitably a powerful figure will appear in your Active Imagination and constellate this raw power drive. It may advise you in the strongest terms to drop all scruples that stand in the way of getting what you want, to drop the commitments and responsibilities that "hold you down." These ideas usually produce a dramatic fantasy of asserting yourself, taking control of the situation where you work, having your own way with your family or friends, making everyone dance to your tune in one way or another.

When this sort of fantasy gets going you become convinced that you are going to resolve all your conflicts, settle everything, by simply laying down the law with everyone around you, telling off those who have stood in your way or opposed you, and doing exactly what you want.

These extremes are so attractive because there is some truth— a partial truth—in them. We all have areas where we have been weak, where we've failed to take a stand, both with ourselves and with the people around us. If we have been weak-willed, if we have been pushed around by our own compulsions, bogged down in the usual contradictions of life, it is not surprising that we get a clarion call from the unconscious summoning us to the opposite extreme. We are seized by a fantasy of what it would be like to solve everything with a pure, clear act of power and will. But if we take this message literally and try to act it out in its raw, unevolved form, we are led to behave like Attila the Hun. We leave a path of destruction behind us.

It is exactly at this point that your sense of ethical values must be brought into the equation. Otherwise you would go to a destructive—ultimately *self*-destructive—extreme. Your life would be turned into a desert, bereft of human values or human relationship.

It becomes the crucial task of the ego to answer back, to speak up for human values like fairness and commitment. The ego must ask, "What effect will this extreme, otherworldly doctrine have on my everyday life?" The ego must find the way to gentle and humanize these impersonal forces of the unconscious, with their overwhelming, sometimes inhuman, nature.

If an attitude comes roaring out of your unconscious that will destroy your practical existence, hurt your relationship with your family, cause trouble for you at your job, or get you into power struggles with everyone, then you have both the duty and the right to answer back, to present the ethical alternative.

You can say: "Look, there are some human values here that are very important to me. I am not going to give them up. I will not give up the love and relatedness that I have with my family and friends. I do not want to pursue some idealized goals to the exclusion of everyone and everything else."

We have already learned that this must be a dialogue of equals. This means that we must not only honor the archetypes who speak to us in Active Imagination, but we must also consider ourselves to be equal to them, morally speaking, and therefore able to take an ethical stance—to speak back, assume a position, make it a true dialogue. We must neither seek to dominate *nor* allow ourselves to be dominated.

The critical need for an ethical sense at the ego level arises from the nature of the unconscious itself. In a certain sense, the unconscious is amoral: in that it is concerned with living out and expressing the powerful, impersonal leitmotivs of the psychic universe. Every archetype, every power, within the collective unconscious, is morally neutral, like the other forces of nature. By itself, it cannot put moral or ethical limits on what it does or what it demands. Only human consciousness can take into consideration other values that should be preserved, limits that must be put on this inner demand or this inner voice so that a balance is struck and life is served rather than diminished.

The archetypes burst into consciousness with all the pent-up instinctual power of the primordial jungle, and like wild animals in nature, they can have little concern with human ideas of fairness, justice, or morality. They serve a realm that is close to the instincts: They are concerned that nature be served, that evolution take place, that all the archetypal themes be incarnated into human life. But how that takes place, how much damage it might do, and what other values might be trampled on in the process—with these things, the raw, primitive archetypes do not know how to be concerned.

The primordial archetypes can be compared to lions in the jungle: When we look at them in their wild splendor, they appear as walking incarnations of nobility. But they are also impersonal forces of nature, each a law unto itself, following nature's impersonal and amoral laws, unqualified by human considerations of pity, kindness, identification with the victim, love-relatedness, or a sense of fairness.

Many of the archetypes that make up the total human character manifest as pure, raw instincts of hunting, survival, aggression, territorial dominion. If they are qualified by human values, by a sense of love and moral responsibility, they are wonderful strengths. But if they dominate us without those other, humane feelings, they reduce us to mere brutes.

There is some truth and wisdom in every figure who comes to us in Active Imagination. Usually each brings a wisdom that we specifically need in order to compensate the one-sidedness of our egos and our habitual ways of looking at life. But the more completely an inner figure is identified with a pure archetype, the more certainly will it take a polarized viewpoint, present an extreme that is outside the bounds of ordinary humanness and common sense.

The critical task that each of us has, therefore, when we "take the lid off" of the unconscious, is to think independently and clearly. We must listen carefully to hear the truth that is hidden behind the overblown, seductive, dramatic urgings of the inner voices. You must refine that truth to something that is more civilized, more human, more bearable—something that can be integrated into ordinary human life without incinerating it. And, toward that truth, you must find your own individual ethical stance.

Step Four: The Rituals

To incarnate your Active Imagination means to give it a physical quality, to bring it off the abstract, rarified level and connect it to your physical, earthbound life.

The fourth step of Active Imagination is much the same as the fourth step of dream work. This is no coincidence. We could state as a general principle that whenever you do any form of inner work and bring it to an insight or resolution, you should do something to make it concrete. Either do a physical ritual or, if appropriate, do something that will integrate it into the fabric of your practical daily life.

Since we have discussed this step in the dream work section, we will not dwell on it at length here. You might reread the chapter on rituals, review the examples you find there, and apply them to your Active Imagination.

There is one very important point that needs to be made regarding this fourth step: You must not *act out*. In psychological jargon, *acting out* means, basically, taking our inner, subjective conflicts and urges and trying to live them out externally and physically.

In extreme clinical situations, acting out may take the form of violence directed at oneself or other people. But most of us do a certain amount of mild acting out in our daily lives without being aware of it. For example, a man gets into a terrible conflict within himself over a decision he can't stand to make, so he bursts out in anger at his wife and tries to resolve it by having a fight with her.

Active Imagination presents opportunities for this, because it draws up so much fantasy material. If this same man isn't careful, if he is arguing with his anima during Active Imagination, he will go and start up the same argument with his wife immediately afterwards. He will try to live out the imagination externally and literally.

To incarnate your imagination, during this fourth step, does not mean to act out your fantasies in a literal way. It means, rather, to take the *essence* that you have distilled from it—the meaning, insight, or basic principle that you have derived from the experience—and incarnate it by doing physical ritual or by integrating it into your practical life. You can get into trouble and cause harm if you fail to make this distinction. You must not take this fourth step of Active Imagination as license to act out your fantasies in their raw, literal form.

When this principle comes up in extreme form, it is easy to see how true it is. For example, let us suppose that I am doing Active Imagination and I see myself in olden times fighting my enemies with a sword. This swordplay may be a valid thing for me to do inwardly, but it is obvious that I may not incarnate this imagination by getting a sword and using it on the people I am angry with. But if the subject of the Active Imagination gets closer to everyday circumstances, it gets more difficult to see the distinction, and the temptation to act out the fantasy becomes stronger.

For this reason, I emphasize that we should not use the images of external, physical people in Active Imagination. You should not call to mind the image of your spouse, your friend, or your coworker at your job and start talking with that person in your imagination. If you do that, it puts you under extreme unconscious pressure to take up the Active Imagination *physically* when you are around that person again. You involuntarily confuse the level of imagination and the level of external, physical relationship. You start doing things or saying things that make no sense to other people: After all, they haven't read the script.

Th thing to do when the image of someone you know comes up in your imagination is to stop and change the appearance of the image. You can even do this as part of your dialogue. You can say: "Look, I don't know why, but you look exactly like the guy at the office that I'm mad at. Since I know that you are an energy system inside me, please change your appearance. I don't want to confuse what is inside me with a person who is outside of me." If you do this, the inner figure will almost always cooperate and alter his or her appearance. Then you can enter into your dialogue with a clear sense that you are talking with a part of yourself, not an external human being.

There is also another reason why it is a bad idea to do Active Imagination using the image of someone you know in the outside world. It is what people used to call "magic." It is clear from experience that what we do at the unconscious level is transmitted to the unconsciousnesses of people around us and involuntarily affects them. Even when we are not around them physically, what we do in fantasy and imagination sends out vibrations through the collective unconscious that are felt by other people in their unconscious.

Therefore, if you take up a tool as powerful as Active Imagination and focus all that energy in the unconscious on the image of a certain person, it begins to affect that individual. Even if your intentions are good, the results are simultaneously manipulative and uncontrollable: You can't predict exactly what the effects will be. The other person may feel a vague, unconscious pressure and begin to behave differently toward you without understanding why.

For the same reason it is a mistake to allow yourself to fantasize a great deal about a person. In addition to being as useless as passive fantasy always is, it has a bad effect on the other person, on you, and on your relationship. If we get involuntarily caught up in recurring, intense fantasies regarding an external person, we might be angry and so fantasize telling him or her off. We might take great satisfaction in going over all the sarcastic statements we will say to put the person to shame. Or, we might fall in love, and have a steady fantasy going in the back of the mind all day, how we will court the beloved, how things will turn out, how we will live in an exciting, passionate dream ever after.

First, just as with Active Imagination, the running of continual fantasy through your mind regarding an external person inevitably affects the other person through the unconscious. Second, indulging in the fantasy has a bad effect on you, for it locks you into a certain mode with regard to the other person. You become conditioned, through successive repetitions of the fantasy, to think about the other person in a certain way, to react automatically in a certain way. And this autoconditioning may be completely inappropriate to the objective, external situation.

Therefore, if you have strong inner feelings about an external person, whether they are positive or negative, it is best to begin by doing inner work to discover what is going on subjectively within yourself. Then, if you have anything that needs to be said to the other individual, it is better to say it directly—using common sense and courtesy as your guide. Don't indulge in Active Imagination or a stream of fantasy using the image of that person. And, above all, don't act your imagination out literally.

The fourth step of Active Imagination is a two-edged sword. It is a necessity, but it must not be misused or it can do more harm than good. At this stage we need to use all the intelligence and common sense we can find within ourselves. We must do something physical, yet we may not act out, project on external people, or be impudent and demanding with others.

Finally, the fourth step cannot be separated from the third step, adding the ethical element. For it is your ethical sense that must set limits and be your guide in all that you do.

Levels

It is surprising what a wide range of needs are served by Active Imagination, once you begin to adapt it to your life. At one time it may help you to resolve practical, everyday conflicts, such as which school to send the children to or how to spend your money. At another time you may live out the mythical journey you have stored up within you. At the far end of the spectrum, Active Imagination becomes a mystical, religious experience.

I find that the varieties of Active Imagination fall into three basic levels, depending on the use that is made of it:

1. Horse-trading
2. Embracing the unconscious
3. Experiencing the spiritual dimension

Horse-trading, as I call it, is the most practical, personal level. It is the use of imagination when you need to negotiate with your inner personalities, to make those compromises and trade-offs that are sometimes required to keep practical life functioning. If "horse-trading" seems a rather undignified name for this use of Active Imagination, it is because it is a somewhat undignified activity: It is a blatant process of bargaining with the inner parts of oneself so that some agreements can be reached and life can proceed.

Embracing the unconscious is the level at which we actively try to bring up the undiscovered parts of ourselves from the unconscious so that we can integrate them into our conscious functioning. It is the level at which we are trying to become acquainted with the unknown, inner parts of ourselves. Most of the examples we have given so far are from this level. It is the primary function of Active Imagination, and the purpose most people have in mind when they begin.

Experiencing the spiritual dimension is the level at which one is seized by a deep experience of the great archetypes. The Active Imagination is perceived as a vision and gives rise to religious insight. This is a rather uncommon form of Active Imagination, but it is experienced by many individuals, and therefore it is good to be aware of it.

HORSE-TRADING

Horse-trading is the most practical, down-to-earth use you can make of Active Imagination. It begins with recognizing that you are made up of many parts, that each part of you has its own needs, its own life to live, and wants to participate in your conscious life. When you truly see this, you also begin to realize that many of the seemingly "insoluble" conflicts that irritate you within your day-to-day life are actually simple arguments between different parts of yourself who don't happen to see things alike.

Sometimes, when you can't arrive at a synthesis between the two parts that are arguing inside you, when you can't transcend the conflict, it becomes a matter of interior negotiations. You have to work out some kind of compromise.

Sometimes people are put off by this approach to Active Imagination. It feels too sordid or mundane to use this high art to work out a compromise between the part of you that wants to get your work done and the part that wants to go to parties every night. But the practical fact is that there are times when the only way you can keep functioning is by doing some good, honest horse-trading. At least it sets up a communication between the different parts of yourself who haven't been speaking—and eventually that communication leads to a synthesis.

When I first became an analytical psychologist, I often had to work in the evening. Many of my patients worked during the day and could only come in the evening or on weekends. It was not a bad schedule, since I had my days free, but for some reason I resented it bitterly. Some inner part of me was used to having my evenings free for *me*—for visiting friends, socializing, music, personal life.

This childish part of me was furious. And the unconscious, irrational resentment found its way into my practical life. I was irritable toward my patients. I almost forgot appointments. These are the kinds of things that happen when someone in the unconscious is absolutely opposed to what the ego has set up.

I took this problem to Active Imagination. I looked for that part of me that was angry at my work schedule. The image that came up was a spoiled adolescent. He said: "No! I will not work in the evening. That is feeling time. That is fun time. That is human being time. That is not work time, and that is final!"

So I set up a long conversation with him. I explained and explained: "Look: We have to make a living; we have to earn money, or both of us will be out on the street and hungry—you included. Since we are just starting in the profession, the only patients we have at this time are those who come in the evening or on weekends. That is the practical necessity. It has to be done."

At first he wouldn't budge. I said: "Look, we have to pay the rent."

And he said: "I don't give a damn about the rent. I just want to have fun. And that's what I am going to do."

I said: "But I do care about the rent."

And he said: "That's tough. You go worry about that."

I said: "I can't work and earn a living if you are going to sabotage everything and make me moody and resentful all the time. It affects the patients. I forget things. I put appointments in the wrong places." All of this was true. There was general chaos because such a large part of me was in rebellion against my work.

Finally I got this fellow by the throat—in my imagination, of course—and up against the wall, and I said: "You have got to listen, or we are in bad trouble. Now, what kind of a deal can we make?"

So the following horse-trade developed: He agreed that if I would go to a drive-in at 10:00 every night and have a nice meal and take him to a movie a couple of times a week after the patients were gone, then he would keep off my back the rest of the time and let me work in peace with my patients. For many months it worked that way. As long as I gave him his meal out, and an occasional movie, he was happy and he let me work. But if I missed one evening of our meal out, this juvenile would be irritable the next day. He would make me resentful and forgetful in my work. It was incredible to me that this character had so much power over my moods and my functioning. But he did.

I never admitted until many years later that I had been forced to make such a sordid, mercantile, back-room deal with my self-indulgent inner child. I felt like Faust making a pact with the devil. But in retrospect I have come to respect these kinds of dialogues, these negotiations, these compromises between warring factions. In some ways they are more humanly pertinent than the elevated conversations with gods and archangels. They keep the fabric of human life intact. And sometimes they lead to a consciousness that is all the more profound because it is human, earthy, and immediate.

EMBRACING THE UNCONSCIOUS

Most of the approaches to Active Imagination are keyed to coming to terms with the unconscious by bringing the images up to the surface, reducing the negative effects of their autonomous power, making them conscious, and making peace with them.

We have already touched on several such approaches. The principle ones are: emptying the ego-mind and dialoguing with the unconscious contents that spontaneously appear; extending dreams by Active Imagination; dialoguing with dream figures in imagination; converting fantasy into imagination; personifying moods, feelings, and belief systems; and living through mythical journeys in Active Imagination.

In this section I will focus on two other excellent purposes that may be served within this second level of Active Imagination. I call the first one "going around the walls of Jericho." The second is "living the unlived life."

THE WALLS OF JERICHO

The principle behind the approach I call the "walls of Jericho" is spelled out symbolically in this ancient story:

And the Lord said unto Joshua: "See, I have given unto thine hand Jericho. . . .

And you shall compass the city, all your men of war, and go round about the city once. Thus shall you do six days. And seven priests shall bear before the ark seven trumpets of rams' horns: And the seventh day you shall compass the city seven times and the priests shall blow with the trumpets.

And it shall come to pass, that when they make a long blast with the ram's horn, and when you hear the sound of the trumpet, all the people shall shout with a great shout; and the wall of the city shall fall down flat, and the people shall ascend up every man straight before him.

This story refers to an event that must have taken place between 1500 and 2000 years before Christ, and was at first handed down by oral tradition. If we look at it on the symbolic level, it contains a wonderful archetypal principle—a way of approaching the seemingly impossible conflicts within ourselves.

In this remarkable legend the people came up against a barrier that was absolutely impregnable. It had walls that could not have been breached or scaled by any technology then available to the tribe. But they had a prescription: They had to do a simple ritual, every day, of marching around the walls of Jericho. They made no direct attack, for none could have been successful. Finally, after an accumulation of these ritual marches, pealings of trumpets, and shoutings, something happened: The walls fell down flat.

Our inner lives often feel like journeys from one Jericho to another. We are continually coming up against obstacles within ourselves that seem like fortresses, defended with impregnable walls. Sometimes we call them *autonomous complexes* because they are complexes that are completely outside the influence or knowledge of the conscious mind. We only know about them through the havoc they wreak in our lives and emotions. Most of us experience conflicts at some time in life that tear us apart, that seem insoluble. We can't find a path to proceed on, a place to stand, an approach that might bring a resolution.

An inner problem that looks so difficult that one doesn't know where to start is an example of an inner Jericho. It is like a walled city within the unconscious, a blank spot where the conscious mind can't penetrate, something one can't even understand, much less deal with. It may be that you are hopelessly in love with someone who simply isn't available to you. Or it may be that you have a habit or a pattern that you can't break, that keeps sabotaging your health, work, or relationships. The problem is within us, but we can't understand it, can't get a handle on it, can't find any direct way to approach it.

In these situations the story of the walls of Jericho is a symbolic prescription for a psychological process. Identify to yourself as best you can what the conflict is, what the focus of your inquiry is. Then go around that autonomous complex, looking at it from every angle, pouring psychological energy into it by ritual inner work, circling it like the Jericho of the story until finally the walls tumble down.

The walk around Jericho can take any form, so long as you focus your energy on the walled inner city and do your ritual. Personify the conflict by bringing up the images in your mind and talking to them. Invite the people out of the city and find out who they are and why they are opposing you.

Active Imagination is particularly helpful for this technique of circling the walls of Jericho, but the technique is really a synthesis: The idea is to bring every form of inner work, every method in your repertoire, into play. One uses every technique possible that will give some leverage, that will focus energy on the autonomous complex. One keeps it up until finally the barrier between the complex and the conscious mind is penetrated. We pull the fantasies out of the mind to deal with this problem and analyze them as symbols of what is going on deep inside. If a dream pertains, do dream work; then extend the dream into Active Imagination, and see where it leads.

Let us say, for example, that you find yourself in a mood of depression that has beset you for days. You can't understand it, don't know where it came from, and find yourself taking it out on innocent people around you. This depression is your inner Jericho.

How do you approach it? First, personify the depression. Go into your imagination, and look for the figure, the image, that will represent your depression. Now begin your march around the walls of Jericho. Talk to your depression. March around your depression, and view it from every side. Talk to the figures who come up in Active Imagination and find out what they can tell you about the depression. What is it? Where did it come from? Usually a depression is balancing an inflation. But *what* inflation is it balancing? What do they know about it? Perhaps one of them will admit to being the one, inside you, who is depressed and can tell you in some detail what he or she is depressed about.

In addition to doing Active Imagination, we pay attention to fantasies and dreams. We write down every dream image, every fantasy image, every idea that comes into our head that seems to relate to this inner Jericho. Above all, we keep going to the inner characters, day by day, and talking with them. Pour out your feelings; ask for information; ask for guidance. Offer to sacrifice the inflation, pretension, or otherworldly ideal that is compensated by the depression.

Like Joshua in the legend, go around the inner walls every day. One day do Active Imagination. Perhaps nothing dramatic will result that day, but you have done your ritual circumambulation: You have invested your conscious energy in the complex. The next day a strong fantasy may arise on the subject. Write it out and analyze it as you would a dream; use the symbols to try to understand what is going on deep in the unconscious. The next morning you may have a dream. Since you are putting so much energy into the inner Jericho, you can assume that the dream is probably on this subject, so that day your walk around the walls of Jericho consists of dream work. Perhaps the dream will give a startling idea of what this Jericho really is.

Each day, in one form or another, keep going around the walls of this autonomous complex. Eventually, the walls will come down, and you will begin to see what is there and what is to be done about it.

The principle at work here is one of *cumulative energy*. One keeps investing energy, pouring the energy of consciousness into this inner complex, until finally it has to break. The Gordian knot falls apart; the seemingly impregnable walls fall down. The complex finally becomes penetrable by consciousness. One walks into the walled city and finds out what part of oneself lives there and why it has declared war.

One requirement for this miraculous process is that we not expect instant results. Sometimes results do come amazingly quickly, but remember that you are dealing with parts of yourself that have been sealed off completely, absolutely impervious to consciousness, perhaps for years. We have to give this process time, and stick with it.

In the old biblical story, God instructed Joshua to march around the walls for a full seven days. Seven symbolizes a complete cycle of inner time, the inner time required for a complete evolution of consciousness. Your experience of Jericho will require seven *inner units* of time—whatever time is required for you to open up genuine consciousness of your Jericho. Outwardly it could be seven days, seven weeks, seven months, or seven years.

One thing is certain: If you make a start, and do your daily march around the walls, you will find a resolution in the end. You don't have to suffer passively. You can do something. You can enlist the help of your inner strengths, and you can begin to march. Miraculously, all you have to do is march. You just have to invest the energy, do the ritual, and the results come, no matter how stupid you feel, no matter how weak or incompetent you are in the face of this inner complex. You march, and you march, and you march, and then the walls fall.

It usually happens more quickly than you expect. I have seen people begin this highly concentrated technique with heroic courage, determined to struggle for twenty years, if necessary, to overcome this insoluble problem and see it resolved in only three or four days of intense effort!

But other Jerichos may be more difficult. They are the ones imbedded in the very deep places of the unconscious. They are, in a sense, "life problems" that stay with us for many years and are actually necessary for our growth. They make us suffer, but they give us our maturity and our individuality in return.

For these "life problems" the circling of the walls of Jericho is an exact prescription. If you personify the thing in your life that most afflicts you, make it your "Jericho," and march around that Jericho in your Active Imagination, you will evolve your problem into a source of consciousness and growth. You will learn that some of our problems and obstacles are our truest friends—our wounds turn out to be the source of our healing.

LIVING THE UNLIVED LIFE

One of the highest uses of Active Imagination is to find a level on which we may experience the unlived parts of ourselves.

We are all a rich mixture of archetypes, energies, and potentialities. Some of the possibilities within us are never lived out because they look "bad" or inferior to us. Our egos tend to classify anything they don't understand as "bad," and, naturally, we avoid looking at the things in us that make us uncomfortable. But if we can find our way around our egos' prejudices, we are surprised to find that some of these unlived or repressed qualities turn out to be the finest strengths we have.

Probably the main reason that we all have so many "unlived

lives" is that there are just not enough years in a human life to experience all the possible personalities, talents, occupations, and relationships that are contained potentially within us.

At some point along the way we all make choices. A man may feel he has the makings of a concert pianist, but he also has a talent for business and he finds himself climbing the corporate ladder, organizing his life around the business world and supporting a family. Still, the artist in him lives on as a potentiality that he hasn't had time to live externally.

In the same way a woman who chooses to be a business person may wake up one day, years later, and realize that some part of her always longed to stay home with the children and be a housewife. Or she may discover a part of herself that would have chosen a religious life, the life of a nun or a life of reclusive meditation.

In Active Imagination we can go to these unlived parts of ourselves and experience them in a meaningful way. It is possible to live much of life on a symbolic level, and this often satisfies that unlived part of ourselves even more than if we had lived it out externally. It seems that God and nature don't mind how we live out these potentialities within ourselves. If we live them out externally, that is good, so long as it is a conscious experience. If we live them out inwardly, on the level of symbolic experience, it often goes deeper, is more intense, and produces more consciousness.

Even ten lifetimes would not be enough time to marry all the people one has loved, follow all the occupations and interests that one might have enjoyed, or live out fully all the personalities hidden within. But if we ignore these unlived possibilities, they can go sour. They can assert themselves in clumsy ways. We may sit around feeling nostalgic about "what might have been." Or we can get bitter and blame bad luck or other people for denying us the chance to be heroic, rich, or famous.

Whatever that other life is, you can still live it, if you will consent to do so as an inner experience. In dream and imagination, you can go to that unlived life; you can discover what it would have felt like to follow that route rather than the ones you chose. You can experience both the negative and the positive sides of it in Active Imagination. Very likely you will discover that it wouldn't have been so much more wonderful than the life you have lived. But it is important that you experience it, for all the main energies in your total self need to be lived out in some conscious way.

I know a man who has a very strong religious vocation. Although he never became a priest in the church, he lives for all practical purposes like a monk. He has remained a bachelor and leads a life that is reclusive, spending his days in prayer, contemplation, meditation in the inner world. At the same time he serves a very important function among his large, extended Latin family: He carries the religious presence for them, and he is the counselor they turn to when they need wisdom from the inner world.

A few years ago a very startling thing happened to this man. He dreamed one night that he lived in Italy. He had a voluptuous Italian wife and a bunch of children living with him in a village. That in itself is not surprising, but the same dream continued the following night and for every night, day after day, week after week, for several months.

Every night he returned in his dream to that same village, to his wife and family, and lived the complete life of a husband and father. He loved his wife, fought with her, took care of the children, worked hard to support them. He went to work and brought home huge bags of food on his back to feed his hungry brood. He went through all the joys and griefs that a father goes through in living with a woman and rearing children with her. This continued, night after night, for almost a year. Into that one year he squeezed twenty years of family life!

By day this man was a quiet, retired bachelor living in California. By night he lived in his Italian village, spoke Italian, spanked his children, struggled with the bills, planted the garden, made love to his wife, argued with her, fought with the neighbors, went to mass with his family, took them on outings. He woke up every morning exhausted from his difficult life as a family man!

This man grew accustomed to his life as a father, looked forward to seeing his children every night and having a new adventure. Then, suddenly, the life in his Italian village came to an end one night with this dream:

I am working so very hard again, trying to take care of my family. I am clearing away the rubble from an old structure, a house or an ancient wall, that has fallen down after many centuries. It is an old stone and clay structure dating back to ancient times that has collapsed.

As I am working I discover, crushed under the stones, a very old rosebush. It has been crushed under the fallen stones for many years, and it looks dead, even petrified. I somehow know that this is the ancient rose that grew in this land even before this village was here. It carries the life force and the promise of life and the continuity of the generations for my family and my village.

I sense somehow that it is not dead, but still lives. I take it reverently and carry it to my garden. My garden is a perfect square in the courtyard surrounded by the walls of my house, Moorish style. I make a place for the rosebush at the exact center of the garden. All the people, including my wife and children, laugh at me and tell me I am being a visionary Don Quijote again. They say the rose can't be alive after centuries crushed beneath the rubble. But I am sure it is alive, and I insist on planting it.

I carefully prepare the soil, put the rosebush in its place, pack the soil and water it. It seems that some time passes. Then I see that the rosebush is coming to life before our eyes. It puts out green leaves, and then one perfect red rose appears.

This magnificent conclusion tells us what was at stake all along as this man lived his unlived life in the Italian village. It was the self, it was the wholeness of his being. The rose is a great symbol of the archetypal self, associated in the Latin church with both the Holy Virgin and Christ. The self is the ancient rose that blooms in the center of one's life. It was this primordial inner unity that this man brought into bloom, within his individual soul, by living in the ancient village, living out the ancient role of the family man, bringing all of the disparate parts of himself together.

As you see, this man had two very strong energies flowing in him. One was his urge to be a hermit, devoted to contemplation of God. The other was to be a lusty, red-blooded man with his wife, his children, and the battles that go with that life. He lived out one side of his nature during the day in the waking world and lived the other side just as completely at night in the land of dreaming. The rose, in his last dream, informed him that his night life as a family man had been revealed as another way of contemplating God, another path to the highest consciousness.

This living of the unlived life can be done just as completely, just as perfectly, through Active Imagination.

I once lived in a house on a cliff overlooking the ocean, with a stairway down to the beach. I put on a coat and tie every morning and drove to my office in San Diego. I had a responsible position—a waiting list of patients, a nice house, good friends. I should have been completely fulfilled—or so I thought.

But somewhere along the way a fantasy started creeping into my mind from the edges of my consciousness. I would be standing outside my house and see one of the "surf bums" walk by: fellows who spend the whole day on the beach with their surfboards and sit by campfires half the night with "surfer girls." They drank beer and smoked marijuana, and, so far as I could see, never put on a coat and tie and never worked, never had to worry about paying bills or anything else!

A fantasy would suddenly jump into my head, uninvited, from the unconscious: "If I committed some indiscretion in my profession, I could get kicked out of the church, out of my professional status as a psychologist, and could be a happy, irresponsible bum, just like those guys I see on the beach all day down there."

I shoved the fantasy out of my mind: It seemed too stupid, too silly—and, well, unregenerate—to be taken seriously. But different versions kept coming back into my mind. So finally I decided that some part of my unconscious was trying to get recognition, and I took up the fantasy as part of my Active Imagination. My Active Imagination took two forms: Partly it was dialogue with the "beach bum" inside me, and partly I *went* there, to the beach, hung around with that crowd of young men and women, joined in at their campfires, joined their parties, their surfing, swimming, their sunlit days with nothing to do but play.

My dialogue with my inner "beach bum" went something like this:

Beach bum: Look, you live a coat-and-tie life. You've got it made. You give lectures, you are respected, you've got money. You have a nice house on the ocean cliffs. But you aren't as happy as I am!

Robert: Well, maybe.

Beach bum: Now look at all those guys and girls down on the beach all day. Secretly you envy them. They are suntanned, they lead a completely sensuous, physical life, and they don't have to balance any checkbooks. They are happy. *They* are the really *happy* people!

At this point my respectable world with a professional niche, and my coat and tie, began to fall apart in my estimation. And the dialogue continued—it got worse:

Beach bum: Now, look, just get yourself busted on a marijuana charge, and default on your mortgage payments, and you'll get kicked out of your fancy house and you can come down and live on the beach with us and be happy. You can do all-night things on the beach, and sponge off people, and I'll show you how to make money off drugs; you can be happy like us!

You can see why we usually don't like to look at these possibilities in ourselves! At this point I began to answer back:

Robert: But I like my house on the cliff. I like my guests who come. They wake up in the morning, and there is the surf pounding and it is beautiful. I don't want to give that up. And I like my work: I love seeing what happens to people who take their analysis seriously and make a true evolution in consciousness. I love seeing the thrill that comes to people when they wake up to the inner world. So although my profession may seem stuffy at times, it is a way of experiencing something very high, very beautiful.

Beach bum: But aren't you sick and tired of the patients? Aren't you sick and tired of the responsibility? Aren't you tired of listening to other people's complaints?

Robert: Sometimes. But also there is something real and valuable there, and I shouldn't destroy it. And I like earning an honest living. I like having some money in the bank, being able to help out a friend in distress, or just knowing that I don't have to worry every day about where my next meal is coming from. I want to be self-reliant. I don't want to have to sponge off someone or scrounge for my food or a roof over my head.

I suppose that the historian Toynbee would say that here the two great archetypes of Western Europe were, once again, fighting it out on a primitive level within my individual soul: on the one hand, the settled landowner and townsman, putting down roots, seeking security, making a life in a stable community; on the other hand, the nomad, roaming the beaches of Solana Beach, California, instead of the steppes of Mongolia, but nevertheless roving, living by his campfire, refusing to be pinned down to a place, a job, or responsibility.

I had touched something very deep in myself. A part of me wanted more than my coat-and-tie world. I sweated in the presence of this inner beach bum. I squirmed. I was scared. I felt I really was capable of turning into the "bum" I secretly wanted to be! That is the way it is with true Active Imagination. When you come into contact with a real part of yourself, you feel it as a threat, a menace. Your knees knock. You sweat and tremble. But you are safe, because you do all this within the controlled laboratory of Active Imagination. You can risk what you otherwise would not dare, confront the things that would otherwise be deadly.

The end result of this Active Imagination was that I made peace with that "beach bum" side of myself. I didn't have to commit a crime and get myself kicked out of respectable society. I didn't have to insult the "establishment," cause a foreclosure on my home, or alienate my friends. But I did need to see that there was an unlived "life" hiding within me, waiting to be lived *on some appropriate level*. The first "appropriate level" was the level of Active Imagination. But since then, I've discovered other levels that merge with my external physical life. I've learned that the beach bum inside me gets very happy if I take several days off and go out to a friend's cabin in the Borrego Desert. I like in the sun, wander around among the cacti and coyotes, and find myself in a truer, happier Dionysian realm than I ever could have found among the nomads on the beach.

It is this same Dionysian, sensual, nomadic quality in me that is nourished so joyfully when I go to India. I live in a world there that is physical, made up of sunlight, sights, and sounds and the feeling of tribal connection with the people I love: It is a more evolved, more complete version of the potentiality I touched when I went to my inner "beach bum" years ago in Active Imagination. If you go to your inner "beach bum" or your inner "hobo" and give him or her a chance to live, you find eventually that this bum is really a *sunyasin*, a wandering mendicant holy man, in disguise. And the nomadic wanderings turn out to be pilgrimages.

THE WASHERWOMAN AND OUR LADY OF GUADALUPE

Apropos of living the unlived life, I will recount here a legend that comes from Mexico. It is a story of one of the appearances of Our Lady of Guadalupe, the manifestation of the Holy Virgin that is most honored in Mexico. You may find it apocryphal, but if you will take it as allegory, it carries a symbolic message. Here is the story:

Many long years ago a young woman became a nun and lived in a convent. The convent was very small and poor, and perhaps the rules were not quite strict enough: Somehow a handsome young man managed to hang around the gate and catch her attention through the grille. The next evening at vespers as she followed her prayers, she looked through another grille, and there he was again, looking at her with a mixture of desire and adoration. So she stopped praying. She tried, but she couldn't.

After that, all she could think of was the young man: his face, his hair, his eyes. The next day she accidentally, but on purpose, found herself by the gate, and he slipped a note to her: "Be at your window at midnight. I will come for you."

She could not resist. For all her sense of sin, for all her horror at what she was doing, for all her terror of the wrath of God, she was totally in love, captivated. So, she waited at the window and went down the ladder, off into the forbidden world.

For a time she lived in a paradise of romance, love, and sensuality. But the dream turned into a nightmare. Her lover was handsome, charming, passionate—but irresponsible. He didn't support her. He made her pregnant. Finally he abandoned her. As years went by her life became more miserable. She suffered illness. Her child died. She finally became a prostitute. Lonely and miserable, she longed for the days of her innocence in the convent, the life she had lost forever.

After years of this, sick and aging, feeling death approaching, she decided that the one thing she wanted was somehow to spend the last unworthy days of her sinful life in her beloved convent. But how? She could never tell them who she was! Finally she went to the mother superior and asked for a job as a scrubwoman.

She was so ravaged by time and sickness that no one in the convent recognized her. Every day she scrubbed the floors of the cells and the chapel. She was surprised by one thing: For some strange reason, no new nun had been moved into her cell. It was just the same as she had left it years before. Why? she wondered. But she was afraid to ask anyone.

After many days of this hard work, which was for her a penance, she found herself on the floor of the chapel, surveying the wreckage of her life as she scrubbed the tiles. She looked up at the statue of Our Lady of Guadalupe, with her flowing mantle the color of the blue night sky and the stars shining from it. To her amazement and terror, the statue came to life. She saw the Virgin in her living form. The Virgin came down from the altar and stood by the kneeling scrubwoman, who waited to be castigated and damned for eternity.

Then the Lady spoke: "Don't you know that I have taken your place, here in the convent all these many years, waiting for your return? Every day I have taken your place in the choir stall, every day taken your place at meals, and done your tasks. No one here, other than I, knows that you have been gone. You have never ceased to be a nun, and now you will start your life again where you left it. Now go back and take your place that I have kept for you."

And so she did.

If we take this legend as symbol, it expresses a wonderful principle. Whatever life we live in our bodies—whether priest or nun, businessman or career woman, husband or wife, mother or father, professional in coat and tie or field-worker in overalls—each of us has many lives that wait inside us, wanting somehow to be lived and consciously honored.

If you are a nun, you can legitimately go in Active Imagination to the inner world and there live through all the unlived potentialities within you. You may go down the ladder, see what that secular world is all about, and honor it for what it is. For however many cycles of inner time you may be there, the Virgin will take your place for you in your stall. When you come back to your cell, no one save she will know that you have been gone. God understands these things perfectly. If you are a priest, and you need to go off, inwardly and secretly, and live in an Italian village with your wife and children, and go through all the joys, sorrows, and responsibilities of that life, then that is open to you through Active Imagination.

On the other hand, if you are one of those people who live a totally secular life, married, rearing children, or caught up in the business world, you may find a priest or a nun secretly living inside you, an important energy that has been hidden away and postponed. You may go to that inner monastery in Active Imagination and find a way to live out that side of your soul. If there is a great hero or heroine living there, who needs to go to a Renaissance kingdom and struggle on behalf of the Queen, you will also find that part of yourself, and that mythic land where it needs to live awhile, in Active Imagination.

Whoever we are, our ego lives are partial systems, with a huge backlog of unlived life hiding within. No matter what you have done, no matter where you have been or what you have experienced, there is always more.

EXPERIENCING THE SPIRITUAL DIMENSION

The third level of Active Imagination is very similar to what people have called visions. It is difficult to talk about this level. If we are too psychological and analytical, we miss the true power and meaning of this kind of experience. But when we use the poetic and religious language that we really need to describe it, we get mixed up with our popular assumptions about "visions" and psychic experiences.

Visionary experience is an eruption of what the medieval mystics called the unitive vision into one's consciousness. An image or a set of events seizes one through the imaginative faculty with such power that one really knows and experiences the unifying truth of the self. One sees, for a brief time, a glimpse of the true unity, beauty, and meaning of life.

When these experiences come, they always have a powerful impact. Within a day or so afterwards, perhaps one has lost the intensity of the revelation. Perhaps one is back to bickering with people and caught up in the petty things of life. But somehow the memory of these visionary experiences works on unconscious attitudes at a very deep level. Sooner or later, it brings a sense of faith that wasn't there before, a knowledge of the meaningfulness of life that had not been there before.

Such experiences should not be actively sought: If you look on this as something to be pursued as an accomplishment, you are liable to manufacture "spiritual" experiences as an ego aggrandizement. Or you can be pulled off into occultism, which leads away from consciousness and into seeking these kinds of experiences for the thrill or the novelty of it.

It is better just to do your humble inner work. When you have done enough work, invested enough energy into the unconscious, and if it is appropriate, visionary experience will come uninvited. If it doesn't come, it means that you don't need it. This is not a competition for the highest "honors." But since this experience often does seize people who do regular inner work, it is good to be aware of it and be able to deal with it should it occur.

The true form of this level of Active Imagination comes when one least expects it. It is possible to be walking down an ordinary street and suddenly find that the street, the buildings, and the people around you have been transformed into a spontaneous vision. In your vision you may be seeing the "street of life," the whole human race, the creation of God, revealed as a timeless flow of life. The sidewalks and buildings do not physically change, but the Active Imagination erupts on the level of consciousness and produces a vision that incorporates the physical surroundings. They become representations of something that is transcendent and eternal.

One of my patients was driving on the freeway early in the morning on his way to work, with the morning sun rising in the eastern sky. Suddenly he was seized by one of these experiences. The sun turned into a sun wheel, with spokes radiating out and giving birth to all the myriad forms of life and human concerns and activities. His attention was so riveted by the sun wheel in front of his eyes that he had to pull the car over and stop until the Active Imagination finished and he could get back into the physical world again. He knew, as he looked at the sun wheel, that all the separate elements of his life, and all the jumble of life around him, flowed out of, and back to, one source. In that moment he could see that there was only unity and that there could only be unity in all things.

If you *say* these things they may sound like meaningless platitudes, sentimentalities, and clichés. But when such a truth comes up spontaneously from the depths of the unconscious, when one sees it as an image produced from within, one feels its truth. One no longer needs to hear it from others or to try to prove it to anyone. From one moment to another, you know from your own experience.

This is perhaps the essence of the meaning of these visionary experiences, as it is really the heart of Active Imagination itself: It is a way of *learning from your own experience* those profound truths of life that can't be transferred from one person to another with words but can only be genuinely known through one's own connection to the collective unconscious. In this sense, we can only learn what we already know at the unconscious level.

Kierkegaard expressed this principle when he said that no one can give faith to another. He meant that no amount of teaching, no words, no matter how sweet the aphorisms or how rational the arguments, can communicate the experience that gives birth to faith. There is a kind of knowledge and a kind of faith that only comes from experience. We have to look deeply within ourselves to find them, because they can't be experienced secondhand from other people. Each person must go directly to the source.

Misunderstandings can arise when a vision is experienced not as an event in the inner imagination but as though it were a physical event happening outside in the physical world. This was the universal experience of primitive human beings and the traditional understanding of "visions" in centuries gone by. People believed that some spirit or creature appeared to them from the outside. They experienced the images as though they were quasi-physical beings outside themselves.

Actually visionary experience is a form of imaginative experience, another welling up of images from the unconscious. The images are not only projected on the inner mind but become so intense that they are projected outward and appear to be happening physically "out there."

After you have done Active Imagination for some time, if you should experience this kind of vision, you will see the similarity to your Active Imagination and your dreaming, and you will conclude that it was an experience of Active Imagination in which the images appeared to you in an apparently objective way.

The other form of visionary experience might be called *inwardly perceived* vision. One goes through the same vivid, powerful experience of images but is aware that it is happening inwardly, on the level of imagination. You are aware that you are seeing it with your "mind's eye," looking within yourself. There is no confusion, because you don't have the apparitional or hallucinatory feeling that you are looking at an external, physical event.

An example of this would be the Active Imagination that I experienced with my interior lion after he appeared in my dream. At the end, the imaginative acts became visionary in their power. Yet I was aware that all this was happening inside me. Still, the immediacy, the sense of the *presence* of the creature, and the power of the image were so strong that it was almost as though the lion were a physical being.

THE SPIRIT MAN ON MOUNT SAINT HELENS

I want to recount for you a visionary experience that I passed through many years ago when I was a young man, long before I had any understanding of what these experiences are. This is the interior vision that demanded my attention, uninvited, one day when I was occupied with some mundane task long years after leaving the Northwest.

One evening I made a campfire on the side of Mount Saint Helens, where I had spent many happy summers in childhood before the volcano erupted. I squatted on my heels looking into my campfire at dusk. Even today I can remember the vivid colors of that evening and how they thrilled me. The orange of the campfire, the dark blue color of the evening sky, the purple-gray shadows on the mountains. I felt a great sense of joy, beauty, peacefulness—but also expectancy.

A young man, about my own age, came walking up and stood just on the other side of the fire. I was on my heels by the fire; he was standing quietly; and we just looked at each other for a long time. I was still in a sort of ecstasy over the colors of the fire.

Then, to my astonishment, the fire moved and transported itself down into Spirit Lake, way at the bottom, and burned there as a tiny orange speck in the midst of that indigo blue water. Then the fire came back and burned before me. The young man took one step, into the middle of the fire. He absorbed the fire into his bloodsteam so that he had fire circulating in his veins rather than blood. We stood there for some time, I looking in awe at these events, and then he said: "Come, I'm going to show you how the world was made."

We went off into space, at an enormous distance, until the earth and even the solar system had become only the tiniest speck in the distance. He showed me a spiral nebula spinning. This great mass of inert, formless matter, more energy than matter, slowly spun . . . spun so slowly, as though there were all of eternity for it to spin through its evolutions. It spun slowly into coherence before my eyes, concentrating, reducing its volume, pulling itself together until the huge nebula was formed into a diamond. The diamond was huge, many-faceted, with its own light source within, emanating light and color that I still remember vividly.

As we watched, the young man directing my gaze, the diamond began to erupt out of its north pole and absorb that flow of energy back through its south pole, so that there was a circulation of light bubbling out of the top and reabsorbing through the bottom pole. That intensified the color and the faceting of light that emanated. Then it did what would be physically impossible: It split itself down the middle, and, as the entire system continued to rotate like a planet, the two halves began to rotate in opposite directions while still touching each other, throwing off sparks of light and color.

At that time, standing somewhere with this spirit man in distant reaches of space, I did something that it embarrasses me to remember. I turned and tugged at his sleeve and said irreverently: "This is fine, but what is it good for?"

I was gazing at an event of the greatest importance, but being a practical American, I had to justify it by finding a way to use it or finding some practicality in it. Again, I tugged at his sleeve—and said: "What is it good for?"

The spirit man looked at me in disgust: "It isn't good for *anything*. Just watch!" That silenced me. We watched, and I felt that the colors, the light, the focusing of infinite energy and volume into diamond-like density and brightness were etched forever on my memory and had almost entered into the physical cells of my body.

He took me back then, and I sat again on my heels before the campfire. He stood again in the fire. Then he stepped back, and let the fire flow out of his arteries back into the little campfire on the ground. The fire went back down to the bottom of Spirit Lake and went on burning. Then the fire returned. The young man turned around without a word and walked back out into the twilight from where he had come. The vision ended, and I found myself back in my "normal," mundane physical world.

It is very difficult to know what to do with such a vision. I think the answer is inherent in the experience itself: Don't do anything with it. Don't try to convert it into something "practical," or something that makes sense to your ego-mind. Just look, experience, be there.

Some part of one wants to ask: "But shouldn't it change something? Accomplish something? Have some practical application?" There is no need to justify visionary experiences on any practical level. But since all facets of life flow back to one reality, we learn ultimately that they have their practical and human effects. They do change us. They form our character in very deep places. They determine what kind of people we will be in five, ten, or twenty years after the experience, when all of its power has worked its way back to the surface and into our lives. Then this magnificent power is transmuted into small things, day-to-day behavior, attitudes, the choices that we make in the ordinariness of daily human life.

Jung believed that God needs human agencies to assist in the incarnation of his creation. As Thomas Mann observes in *Joseph and His Brothers*, God needed the ladder in Jacob's dream as a way to come and go between heaven and earth. The visions of human beings make such a ladder and transmit information into the collective unconscious of humanity. No "practicality" beyond this is required.

Bibliography

Campbell, Joseph. *Myths to Live By.* New York: Viking Press, 1972.
————. *The Portable Jung.* New York: Viking Press, 1972.
Johnson, Robert A. *He: Understanding Masculine Psychology.* New York: Harper & Row, 1977.
————. *She: Understanding Feminine Psychology.* New York: Harper & Row, 1977.
————. *We: Understanding the Psychology of Romantic Love.* San Francisco: Harper & Row, 1983.
Jung, Carl Gustav. *Aion.* Translated by R. F. C. Hull. 9 C.W., Part II. Bollingen Series XX. Princeton: Princeton University Press, 1959.
————. *Archetypes of the Collective Unconscious.* 9 C.W., Part I. New York: Pantheon Books, 1959.
————. *Man and His Symbols.* Garden City, N.Y.: Doubleday, 1964.
————. *Memories, Dreams and Reflections.* New York: Pantheon Books, 1963.
Hall, James A. *Jungian Dream Interpretation: A Handbook of Theory and Practice.* Toronto: Inner City Books, 1983.
Hannah, Barbara. *Encounters With the Soul: Active Imagination as Developed by C. G. Jung.* Boston: Sigo Press, 1981.
Mattoon, Mary Ann. *Applied Dream Analysis: A Jungian Approach.* Washington, D.C.: V. H. Winston & Sons, 1978.
Neumann, Erich. *The Great Mother.* Translated by Ralph Manheim. Bollingen Series No. 47. Princeton: Princeton University Press, 1974.
Sanford, John A. *The Invisible Partners.* New York: Paulist Press, 1980.
————. *The Kingdom Within.* San Francisco: Harper & Row, Revised Edition, 1986.
Whitmont, Edward C. *The Symbolic Quest.* New York: G. P. Putnam's Sons, 1969; New York: Harper & Row, 1973.